12 POWERFUL MARKETING IDEAS

THAT CAN MAKE YOU MORE MONEY

By T.J. Rohleder

Co-Founder of M.O.R.E. Incorporated
and *America's Blue Jeans Millionaire*

TABLE OF CONTENTS

Introduction 5

Powerful Marketing Idea #1 9
The Only 3 Ways to Build Your Business!

Powerful Marketing Idea #2 19
Where to Find the Best Ideas That Will Make You the Most Money!

Powerful Marketing Idea #3 25
Never Cold Call... Again!

Powerful Marketing Idea #4 37
The Safest and Most Profitable Way to Make Money!

Powerful Marketing Idea #5 47
The "Magic Pill" and How It Can Make You Rich!

Powerful Marketing Idea #6 59
The Greatest Secret to Selling Anything to Anyone!

Powerful Marketing Idea #7 71
*Why the Safe and Conservative Approach
to Business is Almost Always Wrong!*

Powerful Marketing Idea #8 83
Knowing Less About Your Products and Services Can Make You More Money!

Powerful Marketing Idea #9 91
How Debt Can Help You Make More Money!

Powerful Marketing Idea #10 99
*The #1 Thing That People Want and How to
Make a Bundle of Money Giving It to Them!*

Powerful Marketing Idea #11 111
How to Separate Yourself from All Your Competitors!

Powerful Marketing Idea #12 125
The Type of Offer That Buys Can't Resist!

FREE Bonus Book! 139
*50 in 50: 50 of the Greatest Things Learned in My First
50 Years of Life and How They May Be Vital to Your Success.*

INTRODUCTION

12 Powerful Marketing Secrets That Will Increase Your Sales and Profits!

Congratulations on your decision to read this book. This separates you from all of the other entrepreneurs and small businesspeople who 'claim' they want to make more money, but won't take the time to study a book that can help them do it.

Yes, so many people want the MAJOR BENEFITS of being in business – without going through all of the time, work and effort to get them. This is true in all aspects of life. People want THE VERY BEST RESULTS, but don't want to pay the price to get them. **And that's sad because business has SO MANY GREAT REWARDS TO OFFER!** It can lead to a life of complete and total freedom and fulfillment. And finding all of the ways and means to make more money can be a great deal of fun!

So what's the secret? That's simple; just become a GREAT MARKETER. This is the key to dramatically increasing your sales and profits. It's the secret that gives you a MAJOR UNFAIR ADVANTAGE over all of your competitors… And once you get good at marketing yourself and your business, you'll discover that…

THIS IS THE GREATEST GAME ON EARTH!

Not only can learning how to become a great marketer make you a lot of money, but it's also VERY REWARDING and a lot of fun!

5

Marketing is made up of **all the things you do to ATTRACT & RETAIN the largest number of the very best prospective buyers** in your market. That's it. It sounds simple because it is! Of course, like everything else that's most worthwhile; IT'S NOT EASY. This is especially true in today's overcrowded and over-hyped marketplace. But tell me ANY GAME that's easy and I'll show you one boring game that you don't want to play!

Anyway, the fact that learning how to become a great marketer is difficult is THE #1 REASON why none of your competitors will EVER do it. Remember that. Think deeply about that. Then consider this fact: **your ability to ATTRACT & RETAIN the very best customers in your marketplace is the key to making all the money you've ever dreamed of making.** Sure, there's a learning curve you must go through and it can be a bit painful. But that's THE PRICE you must continually pay to get really good at ANYTHING you want bad enough. And I promise, when you get good at all of the things you have to do to MARKET YOURSELF AND YOUR BUSINESS, you'll have a major unfair advantage over all of the people and companies who are also trying to do business with the same prospects and customers that you're trying to attract and retain.

So please **let this be your #1 FOCUS** as you go through this book. Have fun reading and thinking about all of the powerful ideas and strategies I'm about to share with you.

Here's What You'll Discover in This Book

This book gives you 12 of my most powerful marketing secrets that I've used to generate millions of dollars in my own small business. These secrets will dramatically INCREASE

YOUR SALES AND PROFITS! You can use them to get ALL of the very best prospective buyers in your marketplace will practically stand in line with money in hand and beg you to take it!

HOW'S THAT for a great visual!

As you know, every business exists to serve its marketplace. And yet, how many entrepreneurs and business owners are TOTALLY FOCUSED on their marketing? And how many of your competitors are constantly seeking the very best ways to give their best prospects and customers the major benefits they want more than anything else and are not getting from anyone else? Very few, IF ANY!!! But you can and WILL when you simply do the things that I tell you about in this book. So study this book and discover the powerful marketing secrets you can use to completely TRANSFORM YOUR BUSINESS. As you'll see; **these 12 little-known methods give you a very real 'unfair advantage' over the other people and companies who are trying to do business with the same people you're after.** I'll go over all the details in this book. I sincerely hope you'll use these powerful marketing methods to attract and retain the very best prospects and customers.

And to reward you for purchasing this book, I have…

A great FREE business-building gift for you!

Yes, I have a gift waiting for you that can DRAMATICALLY INCREASE YOUR SALES AND PROFITS! Here's what it's all about: I spent TEN FULL YEARS writing down all of the greatest marketing and success secrets I discovered during that time period. Each day, I took a few notes and, at the end of a decade, I had a GIANT LIST of 6,159 powerful secrets! This list is ALMOST 1,000 PAGES of hard core money-making ideas and strategies!** **Best of all, this massive collection is now YOURS**

ABSOLUTELY FREE! Just go to: www.6159FreeSecrets.com and get it NOW! As you'll see, this complete collection of 6,159 of my greatest marketing and success secrets, far more valuable than those you can buy from others for $495 to $997, is absolutely **FREE.** No cost, no obligation.

Why am I giving away this GIANT COLLECTION of secrets, that took ONE DECADE to discover and compile, FOR FREE? That's simple: I believe many of the people who receive these 6,159 secrets in this huge 955 page PDF document will want to obtain some of our other books and audio programs and participate in our special COACHING PROGRAMS. However, you are NOT obligated to buy anything—now or ever.

I know you're serious about making more money or you wouldn't be reading this. So go to: www.6159FreeSecrets.com and get this complete collection of 6,159 of my greatest marketing and success secrets right now! **You'll get this GREAT FREE GIFT in the next few minutes, just for letting me add you to my Client mailing list,** and I'll stay in CLOSE TOUCH with you... and do all I can to help you make even more money with my proven marketing strategies and methods.

So with all this said, let's begin...

** WARNING: This complete collection of 6,159 marketing and success secrets contains MANY CONTROVERSIAL ideas and methods. Also, it was originally written for MY EYES ONLY and for a few VERY CLOSE FRIENDS. Therefore, the language is X-RATED in some places [I got VERY EXCITED when I wrote many of these ideas and used VERY FOUL LANGUAGE to get my ideas across!] so 'IF' you are EASILY OFFENDED or do NOT want to read anything OFFENSIVE, then please do both of us a favor and DO NOT go to my website and download this FREE gift. THANK YOU for your understanding.

POWERFUL
MARKETING IDEA
#1

The Only 3 Ways to Build Your Business!

The Basics of Building a Business

It's all about the basics. Always.

There are so many different kinds of businesses, and everybody thinks that theirs is unique. At some level they're absolutely correct: their business *is* unique, no question about it. But there are common denominators to every business in the world, and I think it's really important to focus on those, especially during the planning stages. **Whenever you get confused, whenever you get frustrated, go back to the basics.** Take a deep breath, calm yourself down, and think about that.

I'll be revealing a number of basic formulas, and the following is one of the *most* basic. I like to go back to it again and again, whenever I get confused about all the possible choices. It goes like this: **There are only *three ways* to build a business.** With rare exceptions, this applies to every business there is. **The first way to build your business is to get more customers. The second way to build a business is to sell more big-ticket items for greater profits per transaction. The third way is to sell more often to your existing customers.**

Those are pretty straightforward... but people tend to screw themselves out of money regularly by not keeping those three simple options in mind. Don't shoot yourself in the foot this way. Start paying attention to how other companies are using all these ways to make money. **Get good at getting on the other side of the cash register,** as we like to say, and realize that all the ideas that these other people are using to get more customers, or get them to come back more often, or get them to spend more money, are all potentially transferable from their business to yours.

Whenever you start thinking, "Oh, my business is different, you don't understand," then you're not being very open and receptive to new ideas. **And you've *got* be open and receptive.** There's a time for shooting down ideas, or for editing them and trying to pick them apart and trying to see which ones are better than others... but it's not in the very beginning. Stay open. Stay receptive. **Look for ways that other companies are doing these three things I've mentioned.**

Now, everybody realizes that you have to keep trying to attract new customers. In fact, that's what most business owners spend most of their time on. And that's great, **but the other two ways are how you make all your real profits, and you ignore them at your peril.** What usually ends up happening is that these folks aren't doing anything special for their old customers. **Therefore, you've got to have a marketing system in place to acquire new customers automatically while you take care of your older customers directly.** You build your marketing system once and set it in place; afterward, it just keeps working for you, with some minor modifications along the way. You can't just set it and forget it; you've got to continue to work on it, make tweaks, change it, and adjust it.

For over two decades now, we've done new customer acquisition on a weekly basis. That's part of our marketing system. Every week, we send out tens of thousands of direct mail packages. Come rain or shine, 52 weeks a year, we've got something out there to attract new customers. That's how we build our business the first way. **The second way is by selling high ticket items.** For example, we've just put together a new coaching program that comes in two varieties. The first sells for just under $5,000. The second costs just under $10,000. Just one $5,000 or $10,000 sale can make a big difference—can pay some bills—and that's important very, very important.

The third way to build your business is to sell to your customers more often. You have to keep re-inviting people to do business with you. Stay in touch with them; you almost can't do so often enough. A lot of people are afraid of that possibility, which never ceases to amaze me. They're so afraid that they're going to alienate their customers by trying to sell too often, and yet very few ever even come close to doing that. Let me tell you this: **if you're not making offers constantly, your customers are out there buying from your competitors.** If you think your customers are loyal to you and only you, you're crazy! In most markets, they're buying from other people too—not just your direct competitors, but indirect competitors as well.

Look: they've got money, so you've got to keep making them offers to try to resell them again and again, even if your business isn't one where there are a lot of big-ticket items. That's the case with our new pet boutique, but we're doing things within that business. We're planning to hold special events on a regular basis—events that can potentially make us thousands of dollars in a weekend, which is a pretty good haul for a little retail store. So we're always asking ourselves: Where's the big payday? Where's the event that's going to bring in the money all at once? How can we pull that off?

You should always be thinking about this. These are the *only* three ways to build a business. **Anytime you're frustrated or confused, go back to the basics.** You've got to have strategies in place for getting more customers, strategies for selling to those customers more often, and strategies for selling big ticket items (or hosting profitable events). This is simplicity itself. It's not one of those complex formulas some business gurus push. You don't have to run this formula by the Board, or get buy-in from dozens of people. There really are only three ways to build your business; and if your business is struggling, you need to implement systems to strengthen each point. When you listen to people advise you on how to fix your business, unless they're talking about these three things in some way or another, they're barking up the wrong tree. **Get more people to visit your store, or get more people to respond to your direct mail offers. Get them to spend more money on you. Get them to buy from you repeatedly. It's not rocket science.**

So how do you do all that? I recommend that you use some form of DRM you can track. It's one thing to hear local business people say, "I'm doing all kinds of things to bring people into my store. I've got word of mouth; I've got my Yellow Page ad, and yeah, I've got some ads running in the Valpak. I've even got a TV commercial and a radio spot. I support some local baseball and basketball teams, too, so my name's on the backs of their jerseys." So they've got all these things going on, which is great—but they have no way of knowing where their customer is coming from.

What you need to do is more of what you know worked in the past... but unless you can track where your customers are coming from, you don't really *know* what's working. So you're stuck going, "OK, I have this all-or-nothing approach. I've got to continue doing more things to bring people in to my business, but I don't know what stuff's working." By using trackable DRM methods, you can fix that problem. **You can know where your customers are coming from most of the time, and you can**

make more decisions to advertise in just those ways. If you find out that these few magazines are bringing you your best response, continue running ads in those magazines. If you find that your Yellow Page ad isn't working at all, well, you certainly don't need to continue running a full page ad, do you? Maybe you can get by with a smaller one, or maybe you can change that ad to offer a coupon or some direct response mechanism that gets people to acknowledge they responded specifically to that offer. Those are effective, trackable ways to get more customers to come into your store the first time.

When it comes to selling more big-ticket items for bigger profits, you might have to get a little creative, depending on the marketplace you're in and the product or services you sell. Maybe you don't have a high-dollar item, but you probably do. If you've got a retail store and your average item only sells for $5-10, you probably have a few things that sell for $20-50; you just don't have that many of them. **Even if you're not selling expensive items, you can try to do things to put emphasis on your *more* expensive items.** What kinds of promotions can you run to get people to always want to buy, or at least *consider* buying, those items? Can you bundle them in a package? Can you run a special offer so people are at least more inclined to pay attention to the fact that you have those expensive items available? Maybe people don't even see them because they're buried in the back of your store. Maybe you can bring those items up closer to the cash register. Or maybe you can increase your average ticket. If the average person comes into your store and spends $20, maybe you can get that average up closer to $30 or $40. Maybe you can offer some add-ons while they're at the cash register. "While you're at the store, did you know we have these on sale here? You can take any two of these for $10."

Lastly: sell more often to your customers. Are you doing any database marketing right now? If not, you can probably increase the amount of times your customers do business with you just by repeatedly reminding them to come back to your store. Maybe your average customer only shops with you once a year, because that's about how often they think about you. **Well, just by reminding them to come back into your store on a more regular basis, you'll get more of them to do just that.**

Maybe you have a newsletter that you send out by email, or even snail mail. Maybe it's full of stories from some of your favorite customers. You have different things that are of interest to your target marketplace, and each time you include a coupon or a special offer that's good until the end of that month. They can come into the store and get this particular product for this price, or they can pick any of *these* items and get 10% off. **Consider some kind of continuity program; that's another way to instantly increase the amount of your customers coming back.** Give them an automated way to do business with you. Maybe you've got a product that could be sold on a month-to-month basis. Let's say you've got a health business, and it's a supplement they buy. Well, they're probably coming in every once in a while and buying... but maybe you can get them to commit to subscribing to it on a monthly basis, so they don't even have to come into the store. Or maybe they *do* have to come into the store to pick it up, because you want them to buy some other stuff while they're there. In any case, you automatically charge their credit card. They're going to commit to buying it every month, and you're going to give them a special price, for example.

Those are the three things to build a business. It's really no more complicated than that, although a lot of people try to *make* it more complicated. **You can increase your business, and build it bigger and better and faster and stronger, just by finding ways to get more customers and by selling more big-ticket items for higher profits more often to the customers you already have.** It's as simple as that. Keep finding ways to make more money. It's out there for you right now, in peoples' credit cards and bank accounts. **You've just got to figure out how to get it, and that's what we're here to help you do.**

POWERFUL
MARKETING IDEA
#2

Where to Find the Best Ideas That Will Make You the Most Money!

Rework Your Ideas

The best ideas are *always* an expansion and combination of previous ideas that have been proven to work. Now, in business, everybody wants to reinvent the wheel; everybody's looking for something that's totally new. **But the reality is that you don't have to reinvent the wheel, and you shouldn't.** I've told you that the idea for our new wholesale printing club initially came from a couple of primary sources; but there were some other sources too. We've got the initial concept laid out, but what we're going to be doing over the next few months is taking the best of the best of every single thing that we know has worked well in the past, and then adding to it.

It's just common sense. **Start with the best ideas that worked before.** If you don't have a track record, you have to study the marketplace. Get on the other side of the cash register. **Stop thinking like a consumer; start trying to think like a marketer.** Try to see what's behind all of this. When somebody is a consumer, their mindset is one way; when they stop thinking like a consumer and start looking around, watching what other people are doing, that's when it all changes for them. Look at your junk mail, for instance, and ask, "What's behind those ideas? Why are they doing what they're doing? Why are they saying *these* things, why are they doing *these* things?"

We're always looking for the best ideas we can find. **We're looking for those ideas that are going to generate millions of dollars, and *those ideas are already out there*.** You've got to believe it before you see it. There's an act of faith that's involved here. All of the money that you want to make—well, the ideas that will do it are out there right now. **You just have to find them, and**

lock into them, and figure out the right way to implement them. And it's always a combination of things that are working for other people. Remember, ideas are transferable, so that an idea that's making a lot of money for one person can make a lot of money for you, too.

There's a saying that goes, "There's nothing new under the sun," and I believe it's from the Bible. Obviously, it was written thousands of years ago. Of course, some of the new inventions just in the last hundred years kind of challenge that quote; but think about it. Even the Internet is just another form of communication, and that's nothing new. Ideas are very similar to that. **Most of today's ideas are really just new takes on old ones—just fresh ways to look at things.** Jeff Bezos created Amazon.com because he thought that he could sell books on the Internet. Well, it's not that selling books was a new thing, because people have been selling books for a long time; it's just that Jeff thought there was a better way to sell them. In doing so, he created a really successful model. Now, of course, you can buy everything on Amazon.com.

The best ideas are just expansions and combinations of previous ideas. It's all about taking something you already know about and finding a better way to do it—like building a better mousetrap. **If an idea is too new, it can just cause you trouble.** There's a saying in our field that goes, "The pioneers get scalped." Those who try to tread new ground or invent something brand new usually struggle with that problem. The market requires a lot of education, sometimes, before they realize that there's a need for something.

Remember when the Segway came out about ten years ago? It was supposed to revolutionize city living and transportation; or at least, that's how it was built up before the big reveal. And what did it turn out to be? A gyroscopic scooter that goes maybe 10 miles per hour. Big deal. It's a little faster that walking. Mall cops and some police use them. But there was this huge hype before it appeared! It had a code name for a while, because they were keeping it under wraps. And then it came out... and everybody was like, "What *is* this thing? What do you do with it?" Well, they had to educate the marketplace on why you would even want such a thing, and what good would it do, and why they should pay $5,000 for it.

The Segway never became what it could have been, because they invented something brand new that was going into a new marketplace, and they had to educate people on it. They didn't do that very well, either. You could create a new car today and put it on the market, and people don't have to figure out what they can do with a car. They see a shiny new sports car, and they either like it or don't. But there's no educating them on what you do with a car, right? They don't have to figure out what to do with it.

New ideas just aren't like that. **That's my point here: that the best ideas of today are reinventions of other ideas. Many involve taking a couple of old ideas and merging them together into a new one,** like this new printing thing we're starting. Printing's been around forever, but we're coming up with a new way to do it where you can submit a project and get quotes back from printers all over the US, who fight for your business. It's a new take on an old idea, and that's what's important here.

So this method involves taking old ideas and coming up with new twists on them... reintroducing an old idea with a new angle, something that makes it new in the prospect's eyes. That's absolutely necessary. If I were to decide I wanted to sell mousetraps, I'm probably going to have to come up with a better mousetrap to get people to be interested in it, because you buy a mousetrap for what, a quarter? Fifty cents? They're very cheap, and they just do what they're supposed to do. So unless I come up with a better mousetrap, something that's brand new and creative and builds on that old idea, I'm probably going to have a hard time getting it into the marketplace.

So take old ideas, and come up with new angles, new twists, a new way to do things. **That's how you innovate these days.** There aren't really that many truly creative new things happening. Even if there were, most people won't appreciate you trying to "reinvent the wheel." People want a little something new, yes; but if you're going to do something completely new, you'd better have a history of past performance to show people... and look at what's worked best for you in the past. **Just keep trying to find ways of mixing things up so that they appear to be a little bit different even if, really, it's just the same stuff that's been working time after time. That's always the safest way to go.**

POWERFUL
MARKETING IDEA
#3

NEVER COLD CALL... AGAIN!

Cold Calling Sucks!

The statement above might be a tad controversial, but it's stone cold true. Cold calling is where you call people whom you *think* might have an interest in whatever it is that you're selling, and you make them a sales pitch. **Well, it's hard to build a business based on cold calling. Instead, you should build a marketing system that automatically brings you qualified prospects who have expressed a great interest in what you're selling, and who are very likely to buy.**

You know, when I started out in sales, the company I worked for expected me to develop my own leads—and that's the way a lot of companies do things to this day. They want the salesperson to make it happen, to go out there and drum up the business… and they know that most *won't*. Here's an example of how that works: a lot of direct sales companies will hire a hundred sales people. They know that their salespeople are going to go work in their warm markets—friends, family, co-workers, neighbors, associates, people that they've known all their lives, etc. That's going to bring the company a little revenue.

Once most of the salespeople have worked their warm markets, though, that's going to be enough for them. They're not going to go any farther. So, the companies look for people with huge families, or who are plugged into a big church or heavily involved in the community at some level. Once they train those people, they kick them out to go work their warm market and generate some revenue for the company. **Maybe one or two out of a hundred make it long-term, and they just keep that machine going; the company keeps hiring people and dumping them out and let them work their warm market.** They would love if those people started cold-calling people, and they hope they will, and that's the only way for a salesperson to really make money in that kind of situation... but they don't really expect anyone to do it, beyond the tiny percentage I've already mentioned.

I think that the days of cold calling should be over, because DRM is such a powerful way for companies to develop leads for their salespeople to work. **It's expensive, but you end up with so many more warm leads to sell to.** In my opinion, **it's the *company's* job to bring in the highly qualified leads**—people who've raised their hands and said, "Yes, I'm interested!" Those people have expressed a desire for the types of products and services the company is selling; they've bitten on an offer that was made to them, which leads you to believe that they're great potential prospective buyers who really *do* have a lot of chance of quickly buying whatever it is you're selling.

Now, in the next secret, we're going to talk specifically about two-step marketing. For right now, though, **I just want to say that when you start thinking about lead generation, two-step marketing is the fastest, safest, cheapest, easiest way to do your marketing.** Think about a dating ad. Even if you've been happily married forever, spend some time looking at some of those ads if you're interested in two-step marketing and the essence of what it is—and you'll see that they're trying to attract a specific person. The person who is looking is talking about things that they themselves are interested in: country music, line dancing, fishing, sports, and the like. They're looking for somebody who has an interest in the things they like; or at least they want to manage the reader's expectations and let them know that, hey, here's who I'm, here's what I'm interested in. Otherwise, they tell you what they're *not* looking for. *If you're a cigarette smoker, don't apply. No drugs, no drinking, no drama.* I've seen the funniest things in some of these dating ads; they really are amusing to read.

The authors of these ads are trying to attract a specific type of person, as well as trying to repel everyone else. **That's exactly the mentality you need when you're doing lead generation.** If you open the funnel too wide and aren't specific enough about what you're looking for and what you're *not* looking for, you're going to bring in a bunch of people who aren't well qualified—whether you're looking for a mate, or for prospective buyers for the products and services you sell. **If you're too narrow, too specific, if you go into a lot of details, then you're going to generate fewer leads—but they're going to be more highly qualified, so there's a process of testing involved here.**

And also, we're talking building a good marketing system that works like a well-oiled machine. **It generates leads automatically, and then those leads are closed through a series of follow-up messages, or by the salespeople themselves.** That's about how easy business is. Now, there are some exceptions; but as a general case, most businesses are all about generating leads—that is, getting people to take a specific action, which might be coming into your store, calling you up for a free bid, sending for a free booklet or DVD, whatever. **The idea is to get a prospective buyer to take certain steps that you want them to take, which proves to you that they really are serious; and then it's just about closing those sales.**

You do that by making people a specific offer designed to convert those leads into first-time buyers, and then it's all about trying to get them to come back repeatedly to do more business with you. DRM is our chosen avenue for that. Even when you do have a customer base, you're still generating leads; you're still running special promotions, trying to get a percentage of those people on your customer list to come back and bite on another offer. That's because you've got to stay in touch with your customers. **Research on why people don't come back and do more business with the companies they've done business before reveals that the number one reason was because the company failed to remain in contact with them... not because of price or poor service.** The customer just forgot about the company. People are busy, so you have to stay in touch with them, keep reminding them you exist, keep offering them great deals.

That's still part of your marketing system, because **all the profits you want to make within your business comes from the repeat business.** You still have to find a way to get them to come back again and again. You can't just expect your salespeople to do all the work for you. **You've got to do things to get people to take that first step, and *then* let your salespeople follow up and work on those leads and close them.**

Now, we'll have more to say about this in the next secret; but the fact is, **before you can build a marketing system to generate leads, you first have to know the perfect prospective buyer you're looking for.** What is it that they really want? How do you reach those people? And how do you cut through all the clutter, all the fog, in between you and them? **Simple enough: you have to develop special offers aimed specifically at them.** You have to realize just how much apathy that there is in the marketplace. The bottom line is people really don't care about you and your company; they're too overwhelmed with their own lives to care. They're inundated with all their own responsibilities, obligations, headaches and hassles. They aren't really thinking about you; **so to *get* them thinking about you, you've got to do things that are bold and outrageous—things that get people to take action.**

Right or wrong, good or bad, in this overcrowded, over-competitive marketplace where there are so many available choices and options, you really *have* to do things to stand out. You may have to go over the top in ways that you might not necessarily want to.

Chris Lakey once spent about a year trying to sell cars. Now, there are a couple of ways you generate leads for selling cars, other than just talking to people that you know. That's the old standby: there are probably at least a few people in your family who are ready to buy cars, and the idea is that if they know you sell cars, they'll come buy them from you. But with prospects who don't know you, there are two things that happen. One is called the "up system," and that means that when someone comes on a lot and it's your turn to be up, you go and work with that prospect. So, you try to be up as many times as you can throughout the day.

At the dealership Chris worked for, there was a system for being up. **After you had a turn, you went to the back of the line and worked your way back up the list; and when you were up again, you took the next customer on the lot.** You just went around and around that way, and tried to talk to as many people as possible. Sometimes you'd get a customer who would be on and off the lot really quickly, so you would get back in the queue real fast; other times you'd get someone who wanted to test drive several different cars, and you'd talk to him for a few hours... and sometimes the deal would happen, and sometimes it wouldn't. And then you got back in line. So, some days you talked to a few people, and some days you talked to a bunch.

The other way was to do cold calling, which could literally involve picking up the phone book and just randomly calling people, saying, "Hey, how old is your car? Have you thought about trading it in? We're looking for some good cars." Or you could talk to people on the street, or in a bar, and say, "Hey, I noticed you just got out of such-and-such a car. We happen to be looking for that kind of car to add to our pre-owned inventory." Or you might say, "I know a buyer who might be interested in that car. Have you thought about trading it in? It's a good time to trade."

When you work your cold prospects, you drum up business any way you can. Like I said earlier, though, cold calling—all cold prospecting—just sucks. It's a tedious, slow process. **You end up annoying people, because they don't like to be cold-called (whether face-to-face or literally on the phone).** It's a bad way to do business, and there are smarter and more efficient ways to do it. That's where this leads to: **building a marketing system that automatically brings you qualified prospects who have expressed an interest in what you have, and who are likely to buy what you have to offer.** As this relates to the car business, Chris tells me that he remembers seeing and hearing about people who were really good salespeople, because they'd put together marketing systems of some kind and were bringing leads directly to them. They weren't having to cold call.

Back when Chris was selling cars, he was just there trying to earn a paycheck; he wasn't really interested in marketing. But he did see people doing that. And I've heard of people in the real estate business who did the same thing. Rather than accepting the traditional way of selling in real estate, where you're just working prospects and trying to build relationships with people and then hoping they'll remember you when they're ready to sell their houses, **these people developed systems for attracting people in the market.** They would run ads, for example, that offered a free report to demonstrate how to get the most out of your home when you sold it; and, of course, anybody who responded was probably trying to sell their home, which meant that you could work that person and try to get them to come aboard as your client.

The main thing here is that you want to create a system that does all that work for you, as opposed to cold calling, where you're just trying to call as many people as possible and get somebody to say yes, or to at least take the time to listen to your offer. This is a system for attracting leads. You don't chase after them; they chase after you, which makes selling to them easier in the long run.

Here's an interesting side note. Recently, Chris had a salesperson come to his door selling security systems; **it was the second time Chris had had a door-to-door salesman come by within a few weeks.** I've already discussed the fellow selling the household cleaning solution. This time, the person was trying to sell a form of insurance, and it was interesting to listen to him give his presentation. In a sense, people like that are doing the same thing face-to-face that you would cold calling somebody. They don't know that you're interested; maybe you already have a security system, or maybe you've thought about a security system and don't want one... maybe you do. Door-to-door salesmen don't know you from Adam. They just go and knock on doors, hoping that somewhere they can drum up some business. At the time, it was quite hot—and I can't imagine wanting to go door-to-door, sweating the whole time as I walked around the neighborhood. **Frankly, that's not really a smart way to attract qualified prospects.**

There's a much better way. You need to identify a marketplace, and how you should focus on *that* before you worry about the product. You start with a marketplace and find out what people in that market want the most, then you set out to develop products and services that give them exactly that. **A good marketing system plugs into that existing market, bringing you qualified leads: people you actually know are interested in what you have to offer.** It's one thing to have an offer that you know that people in your marketplace *may* want, and another thing to have an offer that people have demonstrated interest in.

Oh, you *could* just sell the product without trying to develop leads first. Let's say you had a product that sold for $500, and you wrote an offer and made it available to the people in your marketplace. You would hopefully have a certain number of people who would send you $500 for your product... but starting out, you couldn't guarantee that. **This is called a direct one-step marketing approach. All you're trying to do is get people to buy your product out of the blue, without developing leads first.** Well, a better method is to first attract a group of people who have expressed some interest in your offer. That's called two-step marketing.

Basically, you're building a list of people who *are* interested in what you're selling; and then, from that list of prospects, you develop promotions to get them to buy your products. In this case, it would ultimately be a $500 product, and you would start by getting leads who requested information of some kind from you, who took some initial action. **All those leads would then become a part of a list that you promoted your main offer to. You might have a hundred people who raised their hand and requested information, and in so doing, they became your prospects.** They've proved their interest by sending for whatever you offered: a report, or an audio program, or something else they requested from you for free or at low cost. Of those hundred people, a smaller number, let's say five or ten, became customers by actually buying your $500 product. **You see, your goal is to sell the main product, but first you have to build a list of people who are interested in what you have to offer.**

POWERFUL MARKETING IDEA #4

The <u>Safest</u> and <u>Most</u> <u>Profitable</u> Way to Make Money!

Embrace Two-Step Marketing

Two-step marketing is nothing less than the safest and most profitable way to make money. It's simple: in Step One, you attract a highly qualified prospect. You use a great offer to draw them in, and you don't try to sell them too much at first. **This is how you get your hooks into them: you make it as easy as possible for them to buy or take some other action that first time.** Let's say you send them a free report, or sell them a low-cost widget of some type. **When they come back for more, this makes them feel like they're the ones coming to you, rather than vice-versa.**

In general, that's Step One: getting people to raise their hands. Step Two is where you slam them, as we like to say; it's all above converting as many leads as possible into sales. You're bringing out the big guns, because now you've got them. They initially responded to a small offer, **so now you're doing everything possible to educate them on the reasons why they need to buy whatever you ultimately want to sell them.**

Now, within that guise of simplicity, things can get very complicated. You can spend your whole life mastering the intricacies of this two-step formula, but when you boil it down to its basic constituents, it's very simple. **Yet this formula of drawing people in with small offers and then cashing in later with big ticket offers is responsible for God only knows how many hundreds of billions of dollars in sales every year.** Two-step marketing is very common, and some people are doing it without even realizing it. Any time you do something to try to get somebody to take a simple step that will lead to bigger steps down the road, that's a form of two-step marketing.

The key to learning how to use this method effectively is to start paying close attention to all the two-step advertising that other people are using. Look at the things that marketers are trying to do to get somebody to take that initial step—whether it's to pick up a telephone, send for a free report, or come into the store. This is that first step marketers are trying to get new customers, or even established customers, to take. Start paying attention to this, and you'll see that some people are very, very good at it—while others are applying it haphazardly. **The more you become a serious student of two-step marketing, the more you're going to see common denominators, certain patterns that will help you hone your ability to create your own style of two-step marketing. Your goal should be to systematize all of this as much as you possibly can.**

Take our company, for instance. When business is humming right along, we've got an offer that's out there all the time, generating high-quality leads from people we've never done business with before—people outside our current customer base. We're making them a specific front-end offer, whether for low cost or for free. **The idea is to get them to raise their hands so we can convert them, and then cultivate them as a customer. Whatever we're trying to sell them later on is directly related to the front-end offer they responded to, so it's like a chip off of the bigger block of the whole offer, so to speak.** Once they ask for it, you try to sell them the bigger block. In our current front-end campaign, we're ultimately trying to sell people 300 websites—but our first step is to make them an unbelievable bargain on 50 of those websites. We practically give those 50 websites away, so we can go back and try to sell them the other 250 in a bigger block. So, the front-end offer, the first step, is directly related to the back-end offer of the second step. **The more you're able to marry**

the two, the higher your conversion levels will be.

Your goal in two-step marketing is to separate the smaller list of better-qualified prospective buyers from the larger list of prospects, that's all; and you're just trying to get them to take a small action. You're not trying to get people to do too much too fast; you're just trying to get them to take that initial step. **From that point forward, you're trying to get them to take the second step, which is to buy something more expensive so you can convert them into real customers. After that, you keep making them offers, hoping they'll come back again and again.**

We're testing a promotion right this minute for something we call our Direct Pay System. The first step is to get interested prospects to send for a free report and a free start-up manual. On top of that, we give them a fast-start audio CD and *then* five free bonuses, which are also on an audio CD. So in all, they get two audio CDs and a big package of information. **It's all theirs absolutely free; we're not asking for a penny.** That's the first step: people raise their hands, we send all this to them, **and *then* we try to sell them a very similar back-end offer than can amount to as much as $1,200.**

On that second step, where we attempt to convert the lead to the sale, we'll send as many as 10-30 follow-up postcards and letters. Each will try to get them to go ahead and take advantage of the larger thing we're trying to sell. **To make that conversion, you have to be relentless in your follow up.** You see, most people give up way too soon: they don't spend enough time, money, effort, or energy trying to convert those leads. They think that just because somebody who responded to that initial offer doesn't buy immediately, that person isn't interested.

41

Nothing could be further from the truth! We're living in a day and age in which apathy is alive and well; don't forget that. People are busy. They're bombarded; they're overwhelmed; they're confused; they're frustrated. **You've got to stay after these people and keep coming at them a little differently each time.** With our company, we don't just use direct mail; we also have our sales reps to call them to answer all their questions, to cover all the objections those people might have to buying. That's the one thing you can't do if you don't have salespeople: you're never going to find all the hidden objections that people have. **Even *with* salespeople, you might not identify all the real reasons… but you do stand a much better chance with them.**

And remember: all this is simple, when you get right down to it. **Any time you get confused by any of this, just go back to that simplicity.** It's all about generating leads, closing the largest possible percentage of those leads, and then continuing to do other kinds of marketing to sell them related products and services. Yes, it can be complicated; know that in advance. It's easy to learn, but it takes a lifetime to master, and you may never know everything there is to know. **Now, I don't want you to view that as a reason for depression; see it as a challenge instead.** Even though I may speak with total confidence about the subject, I'm still learning myself—and I love the challenge.

I happen to think that two-step marketing is a foundation principle of DRM; it's certainly one of those areas that's important to your success in the field. There are all kinds of things you could do to advertise your business: different directions you can take, different media you can use, and lots of different options within those categories. **But, the surefire, safest, and most profitable way to make money is to *first* attract highly**

qualified prospects and then do as much business with them as you can. That's the simple strategy here, though again, it can cover a lot of different angles, a lot of different twists. There are many different things you can do within that broader concept. But if your goal in your business is always first to attract qualified prospects and then sell those prospects not just once time but many times, and to establish a long-running, profitable relationship with them, then you're on the right track.

It doesn't always work, of course, but that doesn't mean it's the wrong strategy. There may be times that your promotion doesn't succeed, or when other things aren't clicking; **but generally speaking, two-step marketing is the safest, most profitable long-term way to build your business and make lots of money.** You've got to start by having a deep understanding of your marketplace and the people who comprise it, the problems they're facing and need solved, the kinds of things they want as well as need, the challenges they're faced with; and then you've got to use a great offer to attract them to you and get them to raise their hand, to get them to want to do business with you in the first place.

Earlier, I mentioned our current main offer for new customer acquisition. **We're using this two-step marketing strategy to basically give away something that's extremely valuable.** We could sell the item for a goodly sum; and we know that some people might argue that we're giving it away way too cheaply. **But you see, we want to use an irresistible offer to attract the people that we want to become customers for life.** Since our ultimate goal is to attract the right kinds of qualified prospects for our main offer, we're willing and able to give away those valuable items, *knowing* that we're losing money that we could make on that initial sale. We do have a small one-time setup fee, but everything else is given away free, and we do that realizing that we're passing up on some money that we could make on the front-end... **but in so doing we're attracting a qualified prospect that we _know_ is going to be interested in our main offer, since they're responding to a very similar free offer.**

We're holding that out there to get them to respond right away. We want the biggest possible number of people that we mailed that initial offer to to respond; when they do, they go on our prospect list. **When we market to that list, we know we'll get a much higher response rate than if we made the offer directly to the general public.** Of course, we get varying results on our mailings, and that's always one of the hardest questions to answer when people ask: they want to know what results you can expect from a mailing of a certain size, and we can't really tell them, because it fluctuates by a surprising amount. We never make any kind of guarantee regarding response rates, because we know if we did, someone might say, "Well, you told me that I would get _this_ percentage of response rate. Just because you're getting that, I should get it, too." We don't want to run into those kinds of problems. The reality is that our numbers are all over the place. They're semi-consistent, but not so much that we can rely on them to be a benchmark.

We have a certain number of new customer acquisitions mailings we do on a weekly basis, and when our response rates come in, we look at those numbers. That's Step One. Based on that, we have a group of people with which to perform Step Two, which is to try to get as many of those people to become customers as possible. There's a clever, certainly unique formula for how to maximize your profits using this two-step marketing system, and

44

we call it "meet, convert, upgrade and expand." The first part is to *meet* the right prospects, whether that's through contacting people by mail or with an ad, or actually meeting them in real life if you do door-to-door sales or have a brick-and-mortar store. These are the people who are most likely to want what you have, who will give you the maximum amount of money for the longest period of time.

The second part is converting those prospects: you want the biggest possible number of those people that you've met to become first-time buyers. You need to make it as easy as possible to get them to do business with you that first time. As long as they're qualified prospects, you want to get as many of them up and over the hurdle to raise their hand and make a first-time commitment, **to buy from you *once*.** At this point, you don't worry about building a lifelong customer; you just want them to respond the first time. **Once you have them solidly hooked, though, you then try to upgrade.** Make them your biggest and best offer, trying to separate the most serious prospects from the rest. **Get them while they're hot, and sell them as much as you can, as fast as possible.**

Approach them and say, "I know you bought Item A, so I think you might be interested in Item B, Item C, etc." **You're in a relationship now, so you're letting them know that there are other products and services, other opportunities to do more business with you that they need to take advantage of.** You're upgrading that relationship, taking it to the next level. Once you've converted and upgraded them, try to expand and extend the relationship with the customer for as long as possible. **This involves staying in close touch with them, creating a close bond of friendship, an ongoing relationship where you're selling them**

as much stuff as you can along the way, for as long as you can.
In so doing, you're creating a lifetime of revenue from all the repeat business you do with them. **You're creating a small group of core customers that you stay in constant contact with, because you know you can depend on them to buy what you're selling on a regular basis.** These are the best-of-the-best, your preferred customers, the clients you do business with the most. They're the ones you invite to all your preferred customer events; they're the ones you know you're going to see repeatedly in your store, or who will respond repeatedly to your offers if you're online or doing business by mail.

So, expand that business for maximum profits, not only at the beginning of the relationship. **As you go on, you're seeking long-term profits from these clients.** You're seeking a relationship that continues to be rewarding over the lifetime of your business-client relationship. **Meet those prospects, convert them the first time, upgrade them, and then expand that relationship.** That's a very simple four-point formula for doing two-step marketing. **It's the safest and most profitable way to make money—not only now, but in the long term.** It's also the cheapest way to make money, in the long run; and, yes, it can be *very* challenging. There are many different variations on those two steps, and you can spend years learning how to work it in all its varying aspects. **But over time, it'll become second nature to you.**

POWERFUL MARKETING IDEA #5

The
"MAGIC
PILL" and
How It
Can Make
You Rich!

The Magic Pill

Here's one reality of business that you need to both accept and take advantage of if you want to succeed: **everyone in your marketplace is looking for a Magic Pill. Everyone.** No one wants to go through the pain of tearing yourself down before you can build yourself up again, and the same is true of any form of pain. **People don't want to go through any pain to achieve results.**

So look for the Magic Pill—the product or service that the people in your marketplace *think* can instantly and automatically give them something they badly want. They're looking for this Magic Pill right now, and they're willing to spend a ton of money to get it. **If you can give it to them, the money is going to rain down on your head.** People are going to stand in line with money in hand to buy it, because it's very exciting to them—something that turns them on more than anything else. It's that "wow factor": it captivates their imagination. **It contains the biggest benefit they're looking for, with the least possible amount of headaches and hassles. That's what makes it a Magic Pill.**

My Marketing Director, Chris Lakey, recently came up with an idea that's way outside of the box—something that I never thought of, in fact. It's a way that we can potentially give our pet boutique customers something that nobody else gives them a way that we can take away some of the headaches and hassles they normally have to deal with, especially if we're able to combine it with the idea that I talked about earlier. That is, we're hoping to mix it with a free service that they're currently spending money for. **The idea is to go to their house and do their work for them.**

They don't have to do anything except be home at a certain time. **So they get the very biggest benefit that they're looking for the most, and they get it for free — although there *is* a little condition that they have to understand right up front.**

We're taking away all the headaches and hassles, and those are the kinds of things that can potentially give you that Magic Pill. The Pill will vary from business to business, because of course every business is different. How do you find the Magic Pill? **Well, it starts with a deep understanding of what it is that your customers are looking for, which takes the kind of intimate knowledge you develop during the relationship-building aspect of your business.** Pay close attention to what people are doing. Look at what your customers are buying right now, and follow the money like a good detective. What are the number one benefits they're looking for? Why are they spending their money?

Look for all the headaches and hassles they're facing and work to take them away. Give them what they want, without any of the pain that they'd normally have to go through to get it, and then just stand back. We've actually done this perfectly once or twice. **At the end of one sales presentation, for example, we actually got stampeded.** Not only did people want the product bad enough to immediately pull out their checkbooks and credit cards, they actually stormed the stage — to the point where some of our staff people got knocked over! One of our guys got pushed over and had his finger broken by an otherwise very fine, rational, meek and mild-mannered customer who became an animal because we offered him what he really wanted!

That's when you know you've got a Magic Pill: when people stampede you in person, or when instead of sending their orders in by regular mail, they spend an extra $30-50 to get them in by Federal Express. Or they get in their cars and drive the order across three states to get it to you more quickly. **When you test something and you get three or four times the normal response that you'd normally get,** *then* **you know you have the Magic Pill. This is the reward for all of the hard work!** Look, none of this is easy; if this book has a unifying theme, that's it. And yet when you constantly strive to find that right combination of products and services that just totally drives people crazy, you'll make so much money so fast that you'll wonder where it all was before!

And I'll *tell* you where it all was. It was in the bank accounts and credit card authorizations and the available lines of credit of all of the people in your market... but until then, you just didn't have that vital combination of ingredients that drew it out. **So as a creative exercise, look for that perfect combination constantly.** Ask yourself on a regular basis where it might be, and spend some time really thinking through all this. Creativity takes work; it doesn't just happen by accident. **You get the best ideas by coming up with the** *most* **ideas; and by asking yourself the best questions, you get the best answers.** So here's a great question for you. In a perfect world, if you had God-like superpowers and you could offer your prospects and customers anything—and I mean *anything*—what would it be?

Then come up with the most outrageous answers possible, and don't even worry about the consequences. This is a creative exercise, so have fun! Come up with some stupid, wild and crazy things. Later, when you've exhausted yourself, you have time to think, "Well, I can't really do *all* those things, because I don't really have God-like superpowers... **but what can I do that might be similar?"** If you do that consistently enough, your best ideas will get better. This isn't just some fixed little function here; the harder you work at it, the more you'll develop those skills—those mercantile muscles, so to speak.

We have a program right now that's based on watching a couple of our joint venture partners, and noting some of the things they have that are really hot right now. Well, we don't want to just step on their toes and copy exactly what they're doing. They're our friends, right? **However, we can apply some of their good ideas to our own products.** Now, another case we were interested in was something developed by a friend of ours in Florida, whose product required far too much implementation. We didn't want to go through all the headaches and the hassles and the special software development and website technology and all that nonsense—but we did want the basic benefit behind it.

Through the process of discussing all this, Chris Lakey came up with a brilliant idea! It gives our clients the same basic benefit, but we've streamlined it. **We're not stepping on the other guys' toes; we're just giving people something similar, and they're loving it!** Though it's brand new, already our response rate suggests we might have another Magic Pill on our hands. It's a little too soon to tell, but you never know.

You see, we found something that worked well for other people, then we stripped away some of the negative aspects and the complexities of its implementation, and modified it to avoid plagiarizing the concept—and gave our clients the same basic benefit. Now that we're testing it, we can see exactly how it's working, which is like gangbusters. Now, I told you earlier I didn't like to test... but testing has its good points. When it's all said and done and you put it all together and float it out there, there are moments where you just can't *wait* to wake up and find out how it did that day. So there's some fun to it.

We also have a business within the business that we began about five years ago, at which point we were just raking in the money. I've mentioned this before in the discussion of an earlier principle. This sub-business was bringing in more money than we knew how to intelligently spend—but that was five years ago, and everything changes. Things are slow now; the money is all but dried up, because we've wrung most of the idea's potential out of our list. **We're living in the desert now... but we've found a new way to profit on the idea, and we're in the process of developing that, too.**

Now we're able to give this thing away absolutely free. Well, it's not absolute: there *is* a condition attached, which the customers know upfront. We're not trying to hide it; that's where you run into problems, by initially getting people excited but then making them hate your guts because they find out that there are all kind of catches and gimmicks and tricks and fine print involved. In any case, we're able to give away free what we used to charge for five years ago, when we were rolling in the dough because we were charging for this thing.

Everybody is looking for a Magic Pill—and you have to realize that what that pill is varies according to your business, and who you're serving. The Magic Pill in my marketplace may be different from the magic pill in yours. **Just realize that your prospects are always looking for whatever it is that's going to give them what they want the very most.** That's what you need to look for and respond to, and it all derives from a basic strategy I've talked about over and over again throughout this book: you absolutely have to understand your marketplace at a visceral level.

Such an understanding is much more important than any product or service that you'll ever invent, create, develop or sell. The make-up of your marketplace is the most critical part of the formula, and it's especially true when you talk about finding the Magic Pill. You don't stumble across the Magic Pill by accident; **you have to create it based on what your market most desires — period.** If you create a product or service and *then* go out and try to determine who'll be willing to buy it, you're much less likely to succeed. **Instead, learn who your marketplace is and identify a group of people who are all looking for the same benefits.** *Then* **identify the kinds of products and services that those people want the very most.** By starting with the prospect, you can end up creating that Magic Pill product or service.

Now, obviously, if we had the ability, we would *only* create Magic Pills. But there's this huge gap that exists between what we would consider the Magic Pill, and all the stuff we normally sell on a regular basis. We've identified a group of people that we know are interested in the same kinds of things; in our market, the business opportunity market, people who are looking for a way to stay home and make money. **We have a good idea of what they want, and we always attempt to create a Magic Pill service or product for them.** We're always trying to create the next big winner; but you see, what we think doesn't really matter. **It's the marketplace that determines the Magic Pill viability. We only hit that sweet spot every once in a while.**

You have to ask yourself: **if your clients could buy anything they wanted that would provide them any benefit they were after, what would that be? This is what you're trying to get at in your business.** If money was no object, if skill sets and abilities were no object, if they were able to spend whatever it took to buy this item of yours that would provide this benefit... well, what would that be? What would it look like? **That, of course, becomes the Magic Pill.** What the answer is depends on your marketplace. If you serve the diet industry, then the Magic Pill is probably something that makes people lose weight with ease, makes them feel better, makes them fit. If you really had something where all they had to do was sit back and eat whatever they wanted and wake up tomorrow 30 pounds lighter... well, they'd probably pay whatever you're asking, because they really want that benefit, especially if it comes with washboard abs.

In the business opportunity marketplace, most people are looking to either quit their jobs or to supplement their income somehow. Most want to live the entrepreneurial lifestyle, or at least the entrepreneurial lifestyle they perceive—which is basically the lifestyle of not having to work a day in their lives. They want to sit on the beach at the edge of the water, and sip whatever their favorite drink is while watching the sunset. **They want residual income, so that they don't have to actually do anything else to get it.** And if such a thing existed, they would pay whatever price you were asking to receive that benefit. That's the ultimate dream in this marketplace.

Other marketplaces have their own dreams and wishes—things where people are willing to spend whatever amount of money is necessary in order to achieve that result. **Generally speaking, unfortunately, the reason we call it a Magic Pill in the first place is because such a thing doesn't really exist.** In our marketplace, people typically over-simplify what it takes to be successful and have a business that can bring you a lifetime of residual income. They don't really want to put in the time and energy it takes to build such a business, either. People are just as fantasy-prone in the weight-loss industry. Until science comes up with a workable shortcut—and it may—people who want to lose weight will still have to commit to dieting and a rigorous exercise regime no matter what.

A Magic Pill is what you get in a perfect world, when you can create exactly what people want. That's exceedingly rare, but you *can* create the next best thing. **Usually, you can't give people exactly what they want, because it's not practical or it's too expensive.** Sometimes it's physically impossible. You can't really build a time machine, for example. **Therefore, usually there *is* no true Magic Pill—but you want to use that as a reference point, so you can get as close as you can.** That's why you go through testing, through the trial-and-error process. Sometimes things work; sometimes they don't. Occasionally you hit the right combination, the one-two punch that gives you just the right combination of what they're looking for, and your sales and profits will shoot through the roof.

But even that doesn't last forever. Eventually it dies out and you're back to the drawing board, starting the process all over again. **It's a constant game of trying to get inside the heads of your prospects, figuring out what they want the very most, and then trying to find as many ways as possible to give that to them.** And here's something you have to wrap your head around: sometimes what they want the most isn't what you want to give them, or what you think they should want. But that doesn't matter! **You've got to think about what *they* want.** Sometimes the dumbest ideas are the ones that work the best, emotionally. It's not always the good thing that drives your customers crazy.

It's all about serving customers, giving them the things they want—as long as you stay within legal boundaries, of

course. Do that properly and consistently, and you're likely to eventually find that Magic Pill that results in paydays where the money just comes rolling in effortlessly, because you finally found that right combination. It's like a giant safe where you get all the dials to click just right—and then you can open up the door, and the money just spills out.

POWERFUL MARKETING IDEA
#6

The Greatest Secret to Selling Anything to Anyone!

Stories Sell!

You have to create powerful stories to captivate your prospects and customers. **These stories about you, your company, your products and your services will do a great job of selling people on the things you want to sell. But choose your stories carefully: they must sound real, they must sound believable, and they must be emotional.** There should be some drama there: some special secret or perceived benefit or promise to the reader. Stories will help you make sales where nothing else will. **They go underneath the radar of people's sales resistance.** Whenever you're pitching somebody on something, they're trying to resist your sales message—whether it's conscious or unconscious on their part. Many times it's unconscious. In any case, they know you're trying to get them to give up their money, and they're trying to hang on to it. The shield is up! **But a story lowers people's guards.** Everybody loves to hear a story, so you're able to slip your message in under the shield when you tell them one—or over the wall of their skepticism and sales resistance, if you will.

People remember stories. **You can use stories to make the prospect understand certain things that you want them to understand, and you can use them to make effective comparisons between what you're selling and other things.** I'll give you some examples in a moment, but remember this: never compare apples to apples. **Always compare apples to oranges.** In other words, compare what you're selling with something far more valuable; or if it's a complicated thing, compare it to something that they already understand.

Stories, analogies, metaphors: all are ways to get people

involved and interested. If you're telling stories about yourself, it helps to build bonds between you and the prospect. One of the reasons people have so much sales resistance is that they're skeptical. **If you're telling stories about yourself that they can relate to, then you're going to win their hearts; and when you do that, you'll eventually win their business, too.** Stories are very emotional things... but then, that's what we sell to: people's emotions.

In creating your stories, think them through very carefully. **Develop them over a period of time; practice telling stories to other people, and try to get good at it.** We all know people in our lives who are really good at telling stories. Our good friend, Russ von Hoelscher, is a great story teller. Recently, we were in Dallas for a big seminar. All the speakers were there, sitting around the table, and we got Russ to tell some of his favorite stories. Some of these are stories I've heard maybe 20 times; but some of the speakers hadn't heard them, and even the ones who had all wanted to hear Russ tell them again. That's because Ross is a great storyteller!

Some people are naturals, **but this is a skill you can learn; you can get better at it.** And you should strive to do so, because stories can make you a lot of money. I've said it before and I'll say it again: our story, which is part of our USP, has made us millions of dollars. **It's been largely responsible for our fortune, because it's a rags-to-riches story that has all the elements in it to bond us to the people we sell to. Our story is really *their* story, too.** Let me re-emphasize that it's commonality that builds friendships... and people like to do business with people whom they perceive as friends.

So our story about all the years that we spent searching for ways to make money, and how we kept getting ripped off and lied to—that's their story! Like we did, they're sending away for all kinds of things that mostly don't work. They're frustrated and confused, just like we were for years. Not that we've got it all figured out yet; to this day, we still get ripped off and lied to sometimes. But we've broken through that, in large part, and figured things out. **Our story is their story; that's one example of the power of stories, and how they build bonds with people.**

And again, you can compare what you're doing with other things, but not precisely the same types of things. Like I said earlier, never compare apples to apples. Here is an example of comparing apples to oranges. Years ago we had some unique websites; in fact, we were one of the very first developers of business e-books when they first came out. For the marketer, the appeal to e-books is that there's no product to be shipped; it's sent electronically, and that's also how the money is delivered. **In order to explain these websites, we called them "ATM websites."** We told people that they were the next best thing to having their own ATM money machine. And we even went down to our local bank and took a picture of their ATM machine (we put it on page five of our sales letter). **By comparing this new process with an ATM machine, we added a certain sexiness to it, and it did make a difference.**

We've also sold many different beta tester positions over the years. In order to help people understand what beta testers are all about, we talked about how software companies use beta testers to help them get all the bugs out of their software before it's ready to enter the general marketplace. Everything that's software related has to be beta-tested. Explaining to people how that's done on a day-in, day-out basis in the software industry helped them understand things a bit more clearly. **That's one of the reasons why you tell stories: they help people understand and remember things.**

When we started selling eBay back in 2002-2003, Vice President Dick Chaney had recently said some interesting things about eBay. So we used his picture and his story to sell our presence there. **It stuck in people's minds; it added credibility to what we were doing, and they remembered it.** When we started selling teleseminars (which you can't really do effectively anymore), we compared them to real seminars. We told people about all the things that you'd have to go through if you went to a real seminar, and how they could avoid doing all that just by sitting in their favorite easy chair and picking up the phone. **Stories like these make things more clear, and they add value.**

We have a new program out there called the Direct Pay System that I've mentioned once or twice before. When we're selling this program, we tell our story about how people are getting ripped off, they're getting lied to, they're not getting the money that they deserve. And again, we're getting people to relate to us by telling them these things. They're familiar with being treated this way. **This lowers their sales resistance; the stories help them see what we're offering to give them, and helps them want what we're selling even more.**

One more example. We've got a new program we've recently started promoting as of this writing, and it's based on a powerful story that Russ von Hoelscher told me recently in Dallas. Once upon a time, he was at a seminar on self-publishing, as a teacher—a seminar people paid thousands of dollars to attend. After he was done presenting, a lady came up to him and handed Russ a book. She said, "Russ, I loved your presentation. I wanted you to see my book, and hear what you think about it." It was a certain type of novelty book; Russ looked at it and said, "Ma'am, I've seen things like this before. Don't get your hopes up too high. The bookstores won't take you, but you can probably get it in some gift stores." And she said, "Russ, you don't understand. I've already sold a million and a half of these books."

That's a great story! Russ tells it a million times better than me, of course, and he tells it with greater detail, but it's a great story, whoever tells it! **That story captivated me, and we've been telling that story during our latest promotion.** That story is going to be central to our sales message, because it resonates with people. It adds a level of credibility and believability, which is essential in the selling process, and it's something people easily remember. There are many directions you can take storytelling—a lot of different things you can do with it.

Stories are an effective tool in the selling process, and they transcend the media. You can use verbal storytelling, if you're platform selling at a conference. You can tell stories on an audio CD, if you're using recorded audio. You can tell a story in print, on paper or online. You can convey a story any number of ways; **storytelling isn't dependent on you using a certain type of media to convey your message.**

Your stories can be either true or fictional, depending on the scenario. **And of course, you don't want to tell a story that you purport to be true that is, in fact, made up.** Furthermore, a story can be yours or someone else's. The point is, a good story also transcends the selling process, in the sense that people don't hear or process a story the same way they process a sales presentation. If you're trying to sell something to someone and you throw in a story in the middle of it, the mind stops processing what it's hearing as a sales presentation and goes into story-listening mode. **Incorporating stories therefore helps people's brains process your presentation on the subconscious level, in a much more positive way (for you), as opposed to you just spending an hour trying to convince them to buy your product.** That's why you need to incorporate stories into your pitches.

The way you tell your story is also going to go a long way toward the success or failure of your endeavor. Obviously you need to know it by heart, but you also have to present it effectively. Let's say your story is typically a 30-minute presentation. But even if it takes 30 minutes to tell your story in full detail, maybe your best story is actually only a 10-minute story... so you want to cut out 20 minutes. Well, which 20 minutes do you cut out? **The remain 10 minutes is the part that you commit to memory, so that it becomes a story that you could tell in your sleep.** You know what parts you want to emphasize. You know what parts you *don't* want to emphasize. **You want to put your story in the best light, and so your story becomes a condensed version of the real story of you.** The real story includes, well, let's see, "I was born in this year, and this date's my birthday. When I left the hospital, my mom dropped me on my head. I recovered from that okay. Then I went on to preschool. After preschool, I went to kindergarten, and then I finally made it to first grade."

Your story is a long, drawn-out affair, and there are parts that are inconsequential to what you're trying to accomplish in selling your products or services. **That's why you've got to condense it down to the most important parts... at least from your listener's perspective.** Earlier, I gave you a very condensed version of my life, which related directly to the marketplace I'm trying to reach. The larger story, which I also tell over and over again to build relationships with my customers, is all about my life and business and my struggle to find a way to make money. It culminates with my success in finally finding something that worked, and my mission to share that with other people. **There's much more to it than that, but most parts aren't important to my listeners.**

Your real, true story is not you sitting down and telling everybody when and where you were born and the whole minutiae—all the boring details no one cares about. **Your story becomes that small part of it that relates to what you're trying to convey to your prospects.** If you're selling a health product because it helped you lose weight and be more fit and have six-pack abs, or something along those lines, then your story isn't so much about how and where you grew up. It's that you lived a miserable life and you struggled with your weight and people made fun of you all the time, until you discovered XYZ product, or XYZ fitness regimen. Now all the ladies stare at you and you like going to the pool with your shirt off. That relates directly to what you're trying to sell, so that becomes your true story.

With a fake story, you're really talking about an illustration; a parable if you will. You're trying to make a point. You're not trying to lie to people; you have to be clear about that. Jesus told such stories, such parables, to convey messages to his disciples and followers. They weren't necessarily true stories, but they did effectively illustrate the points that he was trying to make. You could do the same to present a point that *you're* trying to make. Your story could be about two guys: one's doing one thing, the other some other thing, and both of them are traveling down similar roads; but one discovers this wonderful item, and the other keeps on going. The one that discovered this wonderful thing, which is related to what you're selling, lived a happier, more fulfilled life than Person B, who just kept doing what he was doing. **That's an example of a story that's not true, but still illustrates the point you're trying to make. Again, the point is not to lie to people.** You have to tell them that this is a fictitious story, a fable for teaching purposes.

You can also tell quick true stories about your experiences without getting to your core story. Maybe you're just telling a story about something that happened to you the other day. This isn't your main life story, it's something you're using to convey your message to them or to get them to understand who you are. **It's just a story to break the ice or help people identify with you—to help them understand who you are and what you're all about.** One of these could come early in the process of selling. If you're on an audio recording, it could be an icebreaker: "Something funny happened to me the other day…" It could be a story to illustrate a point that you're trying to make a bit later in your sales presentation. You've already told them who you are; you've explained your story. **But then, a little bit later in the process, you're telling them something that happened to you recently, or some kind of other story, in order to press home the point you're trying to make at that moment in your selling process.**

Telling someone else's story usually involves a true story, too. It's a story you've heard from someone—possibly a friend or acquaintance who experienced this or that. Or you overheard someone tell it, or you read an article about somebody who did something. These are all along the lines of what I was talking about a little bit ago, when I discussed the eBay product that we created years ago. We used quotes from the Vice President and from other people of authority. **Those aren't necessarily long, drawn-out stories, but they become micro-stories about their experiences with something.** In that case, it was what the Vice President thought about eBay as a marketplace. It wasn't this long, drawn out story; it was just a paragraph. But it effectively illustrated the point we were trying to make. In that case, we were trying to show people that eBay really was a big deal, and worth their time to look at and explore. Using a quote from Dick Cheney was a good way to get people to realize that a lot of people are talking about this.

So you can use other people's stories and examples, as long as you cite the source. If it's not an original thought, just be sure to say, "I heard this story from my good friend, so and so," or "This story came from *Newsweek*... Last week, I was reading about this, and here's what I learned from that, and here's why this applies to you." **Without recreating the entire story, you can read a paragraph or two and cite them, and you're fine doing so.**

Stories are so important, and they can be devastatingly effective. Whether they're true or fables, whether they're your own stories or someone else's, there are all kind of ways to incorporate them in your selling process. Like I said at the beginning of this chapter, there's something in the brain that switches gears when you go from selling to storytelling. **People receive and process stories differently; they're much more receptive to what you're telling them in story format, and tend to believe what's told to them—whereas if you're just selling, people are automatically skeptical.** And certainly, if you're telling a true story, that's to your benefit... though even when you're telling a story about a fake situation, people's brains switch gears. It comes across differently.

So use stories, and they will help you make the sale even when other things aren't working like they should.

In the next chapter, **I'm going to tell you one of the most powerful stories I've ever heard in my life.** So hang on, because it illustrates our next principle.

POWERFUL
MARKETING IDEA
#7

Why the Safe and Conservative Approach to Business is Almost Always Wrong!

The Easiest Thing Isn't Always the Best Thing

The easiest thing that a person can do is to stand on the sidelines and argue for the safe and conservative plan. **It takes a hell of a lot of courage to step up and try new things—but it's the only way to build a business. You've got to be bold, willing to take a chance, willing to fail if it comes to that.** Back in the 16th century, Thomas Fuller said that the first, second, and third most important thing in business is to be bold. It's more true today than ever before, I think.

You've got to take calculated risks. You've got to test all kinds of things, and be open and receptive to all kinds of ideas. We're operating in an over-crowded marketplace that's full of aggressive competition, more so than at any other time in history. As I've emphasized before, I don't say this to be negative; in fact, all that competition is a sincerely positive thing, assuming you choose to look at it that way. It means that there are lots of people in your market, spending lots of money. **Whenever you see a lot of competition, you know that there's a healthy market supporting it. You just have to figure out how to get people to spend that money with you instead of anyone else.** To do that, you've got to differentiate yourself from everyone else. You've got to think differently. **You've got to think *bigger*. You've got to be bold, and take bold action.**

The reason that most people don't want to take bold action is that they're afraid; it's just that simple. Most will never admit it, of course; they have too much pride. So they cover that fear by thinking that being conservative means they're being smart, and they take great pride in the fact that they're always holding back, because they *do* believe that they're smart.

And every time one of those crazy, wild-eyed entrepreneurs goes out and blows up their company by doing stupid, aggressive things, it just makes them feel safer in their convictions. They feel superior as a result, and believe even more firmly that they're on the right road. But they're not. Again, the marketplace is overcrowded with aggressive marketers who are out there being bold, who *aren't* holding back like the conservatives... so they're gaining ground in the conflict. **And make no mistake: this *is* a conflict.** In some ways, you have to think of business as warfare. In a sense, then, you're the general of your own army. **You're the one who's got to be out there mapping out bold, creative new strategies that will help you continue to kick ass in the marketplace, competing effectively and profitably.**

Now, all this does take great courage and great vision; but still, you've got to make a game out of it, too. Have some fun with it. **Make your moves carefully and wisely, and you'll be surprised at how fun and effective this will all be,** especially if you make the best possible use of direct response marketing.

I realize that I'm using words like "careful" and "calculated" while talking simultaneously about being bold, because here's where those words are synonymous. Usually, when you think of people that are doing really bold things, you think of carelessness. But you don't have to be careless to be bold. **If you're trying bold, innovative ideas on a smaller scale, you can be very, very aggressive without being reckless at all.** You have to stay within the limits of the law and certain ethical concerns, and you don't want to risk bankrupting your company, but you still can be extremely bold. Even if an idea fails completely, you're not sunk.

74

Incidentally, that fear of failure is why a lot of conservative businesspeople and marketers just won't try new ideas: they're afraid of failing. Fear is the only thing that's holding them back. But why be wed to something as debilitating as fear? **Even without risking everything, you *can* be aggressive.** Even if an idea does fail miserably, you're safe, as long as you're testing small. Sure, it's still going to be a little painful if you're attached to it emotionally as so many of us are. If you're in it with all your heart, you're putting it all on the line; so yes, there will be pain. **But at the same time you're only going to lose a little bit of money, and that's a *smart* way to do it.**

So don't be afraid to be bold. **Test as many of your new, innovative, aggressive ideas as you possibly can. Test them on a small scale,** and you'll never have to be like one of those wild-eyed entrepreneurs who blows their company up. **In fact, you're going to find that some percentage of the bold and innovative ideas you test are going to work phenomenally well.** Ultimately, it's a numbers game—like drilling for oil. You're going to get a lot of dry holes, but eventually, you're going to hit a gusher. It may take 10 or 20 tries, but the money you get from hitting one nice pocket of natural gas or oil can more than make up for all the money that you lose on all those failed tests.

Even if you're not an oil wildcatter, you have to adopt and adapt that same mentality within your business: **test consistently, and be willing to lose a little money here and there. Your market is changing constantly, even though you may not be able to see it.** There are plenty of aggressive competitors out there who are *not* thinking conservatively, people who are always going to muscle their way in and try to take all the money that could and should be yours. **It *is* a war. It's constant,**

heart-pounding warfare.

As I write this, my oldest company is 22 years old, working on year 23—and yet we haven't slowed down, haven't tried to rest on our laurels. That's a recipe for disaster! **No, we're changing direction right now with some of our aggressive testing—because if it works, it's going to account for the *next* 22 years of our company.** And it *is* a new direction for us, a totally new direction. But nonetheless, it lets us use all the skills, abilities, knowledge and experience that we've developed over the past 22 years. **We're not doing entirely new things, but we're definitely reaching a new market in a new way...** and if we're successful, there's our next 22 years, and it could lead to more money than we've ever dreamed possible! That's the dream we're all chasing, every time we decide to be bold and innovative and test a bunch of new ideas.

So I would encourage you to do the same. Anybody can sit on the sidelines; anybody can be a critic. And some critics feel so superior when they see other people try and fail. But as the great Teddy Roosevelt once said, **"It's not the critic that counts, it's the man who's actually in the arena."**

Speaking of quotes, here's an interesting one on taking risks by a guru named Leo Buscaglia: "The person who risks nothing does nothing, has nothing, is nothing and becomes nothing. He may avoid suffering and sorrow, but he simply cannot learn and feel and change and grow and love and live." I thought that was an appropriate quote, because **the easiest thing to do is to avoid risks... but what kind of life are you living if you play it safe all the time?** That's not much of a life in general, and it certainly isn't when you're in business. When you get down to it, the easiest thing to do is to decide never to get into business because, well, getting into business has certain risks. You may not succeed. You might have people laugh at you because you didn't succeed. You might not make all the money you want. You might end up flat broke.

There are all kinds of reasons why you should never, ever start a business, so the easy thing to do is to stand on the sidelines and argue for the safe and conservative plan. You can always put your money in a money market account. It may not be incredibly profitable, but you're not going to lose your money. It's going to sit there and collect the little bit of interest the bank is willing to give you... so it's pretty much safe, until they start charging you fees on it because they can't figure out how to make money any other way in this economy. **The way you make more money is to take some risks;** do the stock market thing, do the mutual funds thing, buy gold, whatever you're doing beyond putting your money in a nice, safe bank account. The easiest thing to do is to take it slow, take it real easy. You'll face very little risk. When you look back on your life and see that you played it safe, though, you'll realize that you have nothing to show for it, either.

On the flip side, it takes a hell of a lot of courage to step out and try new things. But this is the *only* way to build your businesses. You must be bold. You need the courage to move beyond your comfort zone, to go into places where you've never gone before. T.S. Eliot once said, "Only those who risk going too far can possibly find out how far one can go." **If you never experience life out on the edge, how do you know where the edge is?** How can you know how far you can go? If you play it safe all the time, you never know what you might have become, what you could have been.

There's a movie called *Facing the Giants*. It wasn't a big blockbuster hit or anything, but it's a nice little movie about facing and overcoming your fears. In the movie there's a particularly moving scene. It's about a football team, and the coach feels like he's not getting a 100% effort out of his players as they're preparing for their next opponent. In fact, he feels like they're not giving any kind of solid effort at all. So he has them do these drills where the linemen—the bigger, and heavier, and stronger guys—get down on the ground on their hands and their feet, but not their knees. Next, the lighter guys lie down on the heavier players' backs with their feet in the air, so they're back-to-back, basically. The guy on top puts his hands back over his head and holds on to the shoulder pads of the guy on the ground.

So if you can picture this, the one guy is on the ground, on just on his hands and feet—not his knees. The other guy is on his back, back to back, with his feet up in the air a little, his knees above his chest, holding on. The guy on the ground has, say, 150-170 pounds on his back—and he has to crawl along without his knees touching the ground, going as far as he can. These football players are strong, toughened by all kinds of strength conditioning, and so they should be able to go quite a ways, right? But they didn't get that far: some of them made it 10 yards or so. Of course, once they collapse, that's it, the drill is over.

Well, the coach didn't feel like he got enough effort out of them. They were trying... but they were also complaining about how they were going to get slaughtered in this football game that was coming up against a team that was bigger, faster, and stronger than them. He just said, "Guys, I don't feel like you're giving me all that you could be giving. How do you expect to compete Friday night when you aren't even giving me all you've got here in practice?" And then he calls one of his team leaders over, and he gets him down on the ground again and says that he wants him to do it again... except this time, he wants him to give it all he's got. And he wants him to not give up, to just keep pushing through.

He blindfolds the player, because he wants him to be unable to see how far he's gone... **because the fear is that if he *knows* how far he's gone, he'll be more willing to just give up whenever he feels he's gone far enough.** The coach asks him something like, "Can you give me 30 yards?" And he says, "I think I can." And the coach responds, "No, I want you to give me 30. I want you to give me *50*." I don't recall how the conversation goes, exactly, but he basically says, **"I don't want you to stop. I want you to go as far as you can."** And so the whole drill starts over, and the player gets to the 10 yards that he wanted. You can already tell he's pretty tired, but he keeps going.

He's inching along, he's scooting forward, and of course this guy is on his back, and he keeps pushing. The coach is down on the ground right next to him, just cheering him on, hitting the ground and saying, "One more yard. One more yard," trying to get as much out of him as he can possibly can. This scene seems like it takes forever. He keeps saying, "Just give me one more yard. Keep pushing as far as you can. Don't give up. Don't quit now."

Eventually the player collapses, and the coach takes the blindfold off, and he's gone all 100 yards.

The moral of the story is that the player *wasn't* giving everything he had at first. He didn't even know he'd be able to go 100 yards, because he'd never tried to go anywhere near that. **But by pushing as far as he possibly could, until he physically could not go any farther, he was able to realize how far he *could* go.** He had to push his way through the uncertainty and lack of understanding of his own limits.

I think that's what this strategy is all about. **It's about having the guts that it takes to push through and be bold and go where you didn't even realize that you *can* go.**

There's one more quote that I'll read here, from a gentleman named Andre Malraux, a French historian. He said, "Often the difference between a successful person and a failure is not that one has better abilities or ideas, but the courage that one has to bet on one's ideas, to take a calculated risk—and to act." What Malraux is saying is that it's not about skill, it's not about having better abilities or better ideas, it's not about being smarter— **it's about having the courage to think that you have it all figured out, at least enough to take that calculated risk and to act on it.**

And he *does* say "calculated risk," a point which you should keep in mind. In business, you don't want to take stupid risks. That's like going to Vegas and throwing all your money down on red or black, or odd or even, or whatever. That's taking a foolish risk. It may pay off in the end, but it's just as likely not to. You want to take calculated risks, but you have to take those risks no less. And so as Malraux said, **you've got to be willing to decide that your ideas are at least worth taking a risk on, and to put it all out there, and go as far as you can go, and push yourself beyond your comfort zone until it hurts so bad that you have to quit.**

And sure, that was in a football movie—but you can apply the concept to business, too. You may ask yourself, "What's quitting? How do I push myself until I break?" Well, I don't know what that is for you. It may mean that you "fail" in some fashion; you don't receive the results you were looking for, maybe, or your promotions don't work like you want them to. Hopefully, it doesn't mean bankruptcy and the collapse of your personal economic situation... but in some cases, it might. A lot of successful business people went bankrupt one or more times before they succeeded. Certainly, they had many failures before they failed their way to success, and achieved the results that really set them apart in the industry or made people stand up and take notice. **So it's pushing yourself beyond what you're comfortable doing, taking those extra calculated risks to try new things.** You've got to do things you've been unable to do before, or push your business into the areas you've never ventured into before. Push the envelope, and see where the results take you.

Again, as T.S. Eliot said, "Only those who risk going too far can possibly find out how far they can go." **Until you've pushed yourself, you never know how far you can go. That's really what this is about.** It's easiest to just stand on the sidelines, play it safe, play it conservative. But the ones who achieve the best results, the ones who break through, are the ones who push the envelope all the way. They push until they break. They push until they can't push anymore, and that sets the new barriers. That's the goal for the next time. So choose. Do you want to sit on the sidelines? **Do you want to play it safe... or do you want to push the envelope and go all out and try to build the best business you can?**

I know the path I've chosen, and it's the path I recommend for you as well. As William Blake said, "The road to excess leads to enlightenment." **As long as you keep pushing yourself, your best is going to continue to get better. As long as you test enough new ideas, you're going to become more innovative.** You're going to keep your company alive as it goes through all its inevitable changes, and you'll stay on top of it all instead of going under like so many other people do. That's the bottom line here.

POWERFUL
MARKETING IDEA
#8

Knowing LESS About Your Products and Services Can Make You MORE Money!

Develop Your Prospect Knowledge First

Every salesperson is trained in extensive product knowledge. Forget that! *Prospect* **knowledge is more important than product knowledge. Always. Prospects buy perceived benefits and results;** they don't buy products for the sake of buying products. Think about that. **The market comes first; the product evolves from and revolves around the people in your marketplace. It starts and ends with them.**

So sit down and ask yourself the questions: who are the best prospective buyers in my market? What are they really looking for? What do they want more than anything else? Why are they buying the kinds of products that my competitors are selling, or the kinds of items that I've sold in the past? If you've been in business for a while, ask yourself, What are my best-selling items? What do people want more of? What aren't they getting?

We use something called the "perfect world scenario" when we're brainstorming ideas. **Ask yourself: In a perfect world, if I had godlike superpowers and could come up with exactly what people wanted to buy, what would that be?** Then you brainstorm with all kinds of crazy answers—even ones that seem impossible to provide at first glance. The ideas may seem crazy, but those crazy answers often lead to the truth.

In our particular market, right or wrong, good or bad, what people really want is an investment. Well, we don't sell investments; we're not licensed to do so. We sell business opportunities. **But still, what the people in the opportunity market *really* want is an investment opportunity, because the flat truth of the matter is that the large majority of the people in this marketplace at this particular time want somebody else to do it all for them.** I'm not being judgmental here, just recognizing the reality of the situation. If we really did live in a perfect world, and if we had godlike superpowers, we could give them precisely what they want. We'd give them an investment where they could put in $1,000, and then let us take care of everything—and they could more than double that money in a short time. And so, **we try to develop business opportunities that provide those benefits,** even though we absolutely, positively don't sell investments or securities or anything of that nature.

Remember: the prospects always come first. **What do they really, really want?**

You need to try to give exactly that to them, even if, on the face of it, it doesn't seem realistic. I'm not saying that you should lie; just be very cognizant of this fact, and be sure that you can offer your prospects what they want in a way that they can accept. Back in 1997, we had our very first $5,000 seminar. We were really scared, too: we'd never sold a seminar on our own for that much. So we were upstairs planning things out before the seminar and somebody said, "Look, let's not talk about all this 'get rich quick' stuff. Let's tell people that the first year, they can make $50,000 a year. The next year, they can double that. The next year they can double *that*—and ultimately they can make millions of dollars over a longer period of time."

We all decided, "You know what? That's the way to go. Let's just be real. Let's be reasonable with these people." So we went downstairs and opened up the seminar, with over 100 people in the audience. They've all paid $5,000 to be there; and I got up on stage and asked, "Okay! Who here wants to make $50,000 in your first year?" Well, you could have heard a pin drop. The vibes were just so thick; people were like the deer in the headlights. They were just totally freaked out. After a few seconds of very uncomfortable silence, I came to my senses and asked enthusiastically, "Who here wants to make millions of dollars?" And everybody just jumped up and started shouting.

That's how we began the seminar. It was party time! **They all wanted to make millions of dollars, and the truth was, they *could* do so.** They simply didn't want to start slowly. They didn't care to go from $50,000 to $100,000, to $250,000, to $500,000, and then make millions of dollars in their fifth year or tenth year. They didn't want to do anything like that. They wanted to make millions of dollars *now*. That's a fundamental personality aspect of the people in our marketplace. **They're enthusiastic about making lots of money right away, so we have to cater to what they want.**

The same is true in any marketplace. **You have to know the market intimately.** What do they want more than anything else in the world? How can you give it to them, and serve it up better and bigger than any of your other competitors... and stay out of legal trouble in the process? **Until you know that, you can't worry about a particular product**! People tend to forget this—even experienced entrepreneurs who should know better. They think, "Well, if I want to sell this product to people, I should know everything there is to know about it. That knowledge of the product will help me sell it to a customer." That's true, and it's important, but *not* until you're an expert on the customers you're selling to. **People tend to forget about the customer, sadly.**

In a former life, Chris Lakey sold cars for a short while. One of the things they taught him was not to be so focused on a car's features as opposed to the overall benefits of the vehicle for the prospect who was thinking about buying it. For example, if he had a mom on the lot who had her two kids with her and she was looking at a minivan, he didn't need to talk about how much horsepower was under the hood. Now, that doesn't mean that every mom doesn't know or care about horsepower, but by and large mothers are more concerned about whether the minivan has airbags and if it has a DVD player in the back. On the flipside, if he had a young business guy in, and the prospect was looking at a sports car, of course Chris would talk about how fast the car was, and how slick it looked going down the street, and how the prospect could imagine himself cruising through town with the top down and his hair blowing in the wind, and how hot he would look to all the ladies.

Chris would talk about the benefits that were important to that particular prospect. He had to do quite a bit of thinking on his feet, because the prospects who come onto a car lot are really varied. He had all kinds of people who were concerned about all kinds of things; there were many reasons why they might be interested in a particular vehicle.

In any marketplace, you start with the knowledge of who you're selling to, and then you pitch to them based on whatever's most important to them. Those things come out in the benefits that are delivered when they do business with you, not so much in the features of a particular product. Again, in selling cars, Chris talked less about the specific features of a vehicle and more about what those features would do for someone. While you do need to have up-to-date product knowledge, that knowledge truly is overrated; **it's much more important for you to learn who your customer is, and what they want or need, and how you can offer them a solution.** I don't think that there's a better foundational principle for sales than this one.

This does require some flexibility, and as I've mentioned, you have to stay on your toes in order to maximize your sales potential. Let's say you do phone sales. It doesn't really matter what you sell: what matters is that when you're talking to someone, trying to make that sale, you're paying attention to what they're telling you they want. **You know *in general* what your marketplace wants, but in each case you're following their cues to figure out the things that are important to them specifically.** You're using that knowledge to present your product or service as a solution to their problem. Going back to selling cars, if someone said that safety was an important issue to them, then Chris would focus on the safety features of the car, and the benefits those features would have in protecting the prospect's family.

It's not that you don't highlight other things; you simply focus on the things that are most important to your prospect, while downplaying the rest. You find ways to give them more of what they want and care about the most. **It's all about knowing your prospect.** Your "head knowledge" about your product or service is only going to take you so far. Knowledge about your prospects, on the other hand, can take you as far as you want to go, because then you've transcended the actual products and services you sell. You've ascended to a place where you're selling to the person, looking for ways to deliver the benefits they want the most. **Focusing on the prospect over the products is a key strategy in any sales environment.**

POWERFUL MARKETING IDEA
#9

**How Debt
Can Help
You
MAKE
MORE
MONEY!**

Learn to Like Debt

Now, this one may seem a little weird to most people, but to be honest, I like debt. **Part of the fun in business is the constant pressure to meet your financial obligations.** The carrot and the stick are both great motivators—but generally, the stick is more important, at least for me. I suppose different people are motivated different ways; but for me, the problem with all this goal setting that the gurus recommend is that there's not enough stick to it. It's all about the carrot, and the stick motivates me more. **I've got to have that pressure; otherwise, I just get lazy.**

This may sound odd to you, bear with me, and I think you'll see the logic in this kind of thinking. **You see, the more problems I have, the more pressure I have; and that pressure motivates me to work even harder, to do more.** Of course, being in debt, especially personal debt, is just one aspect of that. But it's an important aspect; and when you study the most successful companies, you'll see that there are times when they're up to their ears in debt. Every couple of years, I try to read this huge book called *Behind the Golden Arches* by John Love. It sometimes takes me a couple months to get through it, reading a few pages here, a few pages there. At the moment I'm only halfway through my latest read, and I've been working on it now for close to a month. It'll be another month before I finish it... and then, two years from now, I'll do it all over again.

Now, this is an old book, currently out of print. I hope someday they'll update it, but they haven't yet. You can find used copies on Amazon.com, but you'd better hurry— because I'm buying all of them! So what's the big deal? *Behind the Golden Arches* is (as you may have guessed) the story of the McDonald's restaurant chain. Everybody knows that McDonald's is one of the biggest companies in the world: a Fortune 100 company, publicly held since the mid 1960s. It's one of only two large fast food restaurants that aren't owned by a bigger company, and it's everywhere. **But what people don't know about McDonald's is all the years of struggle that they've gone through.** They almost didn't make it a whole bunch of times. One of the reasons that they *did* make it is that they got themselves deep, deep into debt.

As with cholesterol, there are such things as good debt and bad debt. But regardless of whether it's good or bad, **debt is just a metaphor for a much larger overall philosophy that I believe in: that problems can be good things.** Being in debt is certainly a problem; in fact, most people stay out of debt because it's a *big* problem. But problems are good because they spur you into action—or at least, they *can*. Sometimes they just immobilize people. Sometimes people just freak out in the face of their problems: and they get all depressed and paralyzed. But if you don't let that happen to you, if you take charge of your thinking, then problems are good, because they spur you into action. And life is all about action.

In that sense, therefore, problems are life-giving. Think it through. It's not the problems themselves that tear people down, because as the saying goes, the same problems that cause some people to break down cause other people to break records. **It's what you do in the face of all of this adversity, pressure, and difficulty to counter it that truly matters.**

I'm here to tell you that having an abundance of problems can actually be a very good thing. **As long as you're committed to trying to solve those problems, and you're striving to focus on the solutions, and then you're using the pain that comes from**

all those difficulties as a kind of whip to spur you on, then problems and challenges will help you achieve more. When we talk about being spurred on, realize that a spur is one of those things the cowboys put on the back sides of their boots; they dig them into the horse's belly a bit to get the horse to start moving faster. That's where the term comes from. So when I say problems spur us into action, I'm really talking about something that kicks your ass just a little.

Many people fantasize about having a life that's problem-free. I do, too. In fact, that's the one commonality that all my fantasies share—and I like to fantasize. I've got as active an imagination as the next guy or gal. But all of my fantasies *are* just fantasies, because they lack the one thing that reality always has: problems. **Life is problems. Life is pain. Life is struggle. Life is difficulty— and business is an accelerated lifestyle.** You get more problems, not fewer. Some people want to get into business so they'll have fewer problems! Ha, what a joke that is! It's probably the biggest joke that I know.

Look: if you can't handle problems, and you still want to succeed in business, then you'd better get involved in a good partnership with somebody who can take on all your problems. Now, you *can* do this. There are joint ventures and other kinds of business partnerships where other people might take on at least some of the problems and challenges for you. **But in a general way, business is one problem after another, just as life is.** And with business, often the bigger you get, or the more money you want to make, the more problems you have to face.

Debt is one of those problems that a lot of successful companies have on their shoulders all the time, particularly manageable debt. However you classify it, it's pressure, and the

95

pressure from all of our struggles and challenges can cause us to perform at a higher level as it tightens in on us. Benjamin Franklin once said that whatever is painful instructs. It's true: how many times do you touch a hot stove on purpose? We talk about the learning curve, the painful process of learning anything new. There's resistance, and you have to overcome it. If you want to get stronger, you go to the gym and start pushing yourself hard, right? It's the resistance against the weights or the weight machine or the exercise equipment that you use that causes you to become stronger. You're pushing hard against it, and that ultimately tears your body down... but then it builds you up to where you're stronger than you were before.

So it's not necessarily the stress that matters here, though I believe that stress has gotten a bad rap. If you'll do your due diligence, as I have, you'll find out that people who say that stress is a killer is wrong. Stress is not necessarily a killer. First of all, stress is subjective; one person's stress is another's boredom. **Other types of stress are necessary to keep you moving forward. When you get right down to it, there's no such thing as universally bad stress.** Some people can take anything on. Other people can handle very little before they start freaking out. It's all in how you process your problems, the meanings that you establish for those problems, your level of skill at handling them, or what you're willing to endure.

What is bad, though, is strain. Yes, problems are stressful. Challenges and struggles are all difficult; but you can overcome them if you have some time to recoup, to recharge your batteries. If you're working out at a gym, for example, you have to put those weights down sometimes so your body can recover. It's the same thing with your problems. **Constant strain is what really wears**

you down; it just grinds away at you, so you have to avoid it and give yourself sufficient time to recover.

There really are such things as good problems. **Focus on the solutions and try to solve them, and through that process, you'll keep moving forward.** Some of my best work—my biggest results and best ideas—have come during periods of intense problems, where I've experienced lots of pressure. **You often get your best ideas when you're in the thick of it, when things are chaotic, when there are all kinds of problems and pressures all around you.** That's when you perform at your highest level if you're committed to winning, if you're a warrior, if you're trying to achieve and do your best. So you may wish for a life without any problems... but consider this old quote: "All sun makes a desert." In other words, there has to be a decent amount of rain in order to support life. If a problem-free life is boring, then who really wants a problem-free life? Not me.

Now, I may fantasize about it occasionally, because we all need a vacation now and then. **But realize that the problems you ordinarily face are just opportunities for you to perform at a higher level.** You've got to adopt that attitude and truly believe it; if you don't, you're doing yourself a disservice. Face it: in business there's always going to be problems, problems, and more problems. So change your attitude, change your focus, and strive to solve those problems. **It'll lead to some good things.**

POWERFUL
MARKETING IDEA
#10

The #1
Thing That
People Want
and How to
Make a
Bundle
of Money
Giving It
to Them!

Be in the "Do-It-for-'Em" Business

What do people *really* want? Basically, they want other people to do everything for them. That's why all of us should be in the "do-it-for-'em" business. We started our very first "we do it all for you" service in 2004, and we've kept creating them since. This secret has made us millions of dollars, and it's going to make us millions more. It can do the same for you.

Now, don't assume that people want to avoid all the hard work just because they're lazier than they used to be. Some observers might make that argument, but I believe that it has a lot more to do with the fact that people are just so overwhelmed these days. They're confused and frustrated and exhausted. **They don't want to learn anything new, because they're already subjected to too much information; so what they're looking for is an expert.** In our field, they're looking for someone who can safely guide them in their business decisions.

You have to teach them you're the one that they're looking for, by proving your credibility as an expert in the field. There are specific marketing processes you can use whereby you take a prospect by the hand, so to speak, and lead them through a process of discovery. **You can't just promise to do everything for somebody without telling them your story and sharing your success strategies, your proven track record, and making the case for why they should put their trust in you.** It doesn't happen by accident. But once you've established that credibility—once you've proven you have the goods and can back up all your promises and claims, that you're not just going take their money and run—well, then, they want you to do everything for them. **And they'll basically throw money at you to get you to do it.**

This a growing trend with no end in sight, and it transcends all marketplaces. It's one of the reasons why outsourcing has become such a huge industry over the last couple of decades. There are so many companies out there that will do a wide variety of things for you, which helps the average entrepreneur enormously. This outsourcing trend gives you the opportunity to hire other companies to take care of most of your needs, so you can keep your overhead really low. You pay only for what you need, when you need it; you don't have to worry about keeping someone on staff or paying a retainer. **There are entrepreneurs who are running fairly large enterprises singlehandedly, using outsourcing to handle their needs.** Again, they're only paying for what they need as they need it, so the overhead stays relatively low.

Speaking of outsourcing: I have a love and hate relationship with the Internet. To me, it represents the best of the best and the worst of the worst when it comes to marketing. **However, when it comes to finding all kinds of very specialized suppliers willing to take on a wide variety of tasks for competitive prices, you can't beat it.** It's the greatest invention ever for doing that, especially since a lot of the work is done overseas now. It helps you achieve all kinds of things for your customers that wouldn't have been easily possible before.

We're up to our seventh "done for you" program now, and we've incorporated this concept in other programs as well—like our new "Cash-in-48-Hours" program, which I'm going to discuss in more detail later. **We've aggressively followed this approach**

because it's what our customers want. They want the results without the risks. They want the benefits without the effort. They want experts to take care of everything for them. And so we take all the difficult, expensive, time-consuming, frustrating, high-risk aspects of the businesses onto our shoulders, so our clients can enjoy the benefits. **Basically, our clients become joint venture business partners with us.** We're structuring these things in a variety of ways, always coming up with new facets to try. We keep testing them and tweaking them, looking for ways to improve them. **This processes works best with services, so we often create services around existing business opportunities.** For example, we'll take a Network Marketing company and build our own proprietary marketing system around that company; and then, on top of that, we'll offer to do everything for our distributors or partners. They just can't get enough of it!

So join us! Come on in, the water's fine! **There's plenty of room for everybody here, because again, this principle does transcend markets.** For example: a minister friend recently turned me on to a website called Startachurch.com, and I just love what the lawyer who runs it is doing. His idea is so fascinating that I got myself onto his mailing list—so now I've been getting these emails for something I normally have no interest in. But this fellow is a tremendous marketer, and he offers his various services and information products for two prices: one where he just sells you the information and you can do it all yourself, and the other where he does everything for you.

Even though I don't know this guy and will probably never meet him, I'll bet you anything that 7 or 8 out of 10 of his customers choose the "done for you" service. People already have enough problems in their lives. They're frustrated, they're confused, they're overwhelmed, and this gives them the perfect alternative they're looking for. It's a sign of the times. **"Done for you" is a growing trend**—from the most basic kinds of things you can call your local repairperson for, all the way up to elaborate programs like the advertising and management services we offer or this lawyer's "Start a Church" idea.

People love these services, because they don't have the time or knowledge to do the work properly themselves. This factor applies even at the most basic scale of household needs, not just more esoteric things like business management. Here's a true story, courtesy of Chris Lakey. On a recent weekend, he was watching TV while a good-sized thunderstorm was moving through. Suddenly, a big lightning bolt struck close to his house; the electricity flickered, and the TV turned off. He had no idea what was going on, so he did what he always does in those situations: he tried to turn the TV back on, and nothing happened. Next he went to the entertainment system, where his TV, DVR, PS3, stereo, and similar components were located, and noticed that everything was off. And yet the power was on; it had only flickered. There was no indication that anything was wrong, except that none of those components were working.

So he looked behind the entertainment system and noticed that his surge protector was also off. After testing the surge protector, Chris came to the conclusion that something must have happened to the electrical outlet. He noticed that something plugged in across the room in one of the other outlets was working, so he thought, *Well, maybe a breaker blew.* So he checked the breaker box, and found that all the outlets in the room were tied into the same breaker, so he assumed it wasn't the breaker—that something wasn't right with that one electrical outlet. So he ran an extension cord and plugged all the entertainment system components into another outlet in that room, and everything came back on, working fine. He was certain, then, that the outlet was out.

This happened on Friday night, so on Saturday Chris went to the hardware store and asked about replacing that outlet, and they pointed him to the right area. He discovered that the new outlet he needed to replace the fried one cost just 59 cents. So for about $1.20, he got two outlets. Now, he hasn't replaced the fried one yet because he's a little nervous about doing so, and he's no electrician; he plans to call one in and have him do it. This is great example of why "done for you" is so powerful. The part required to fix the electrical outlet cost 59 cents... and yet, Chris is tempted to pay someone else at least hundred times that amount to replace it. Admittedly, there's some risk involved; electricity is nasty stuff. But there's that part of him that goes, "Wow, I just paid 59 cents for this part, and I'm probably going to pay a hundred bucks to have an electrician come out and install it..." So he may still end up doing it himself, after all; he thinks he can manage it without electrocuting himself.

Chris also has a deck that needs to be stained. He *could* do it himself, he says, but he's definitely calling someone else out to do it. He also needs to repaint his living room... but he's going to use someone else, because it has high, vaulted ceilings, especially over the staircase, and he doesn't want to deal with having to buy a really tall ladder and all the other hassles that come with it. And he hates painting, anyway!

Those are just a few everyday examples of how the "done for you" mentality arises in real life. That segment of any industry is always going be highly profitable. These days, more and more people just want someone who's an expert to take care of whatever's gone wrong. **They want to know that someone else will do everything for them, and do a good job of it—and that they don't have to worry about it.** I think you'll see this playing out in your own life and experiences, if you think about it. There are probably plenty of things that you just don't want to do. It may be that you *can* do them, but you'd rather let someone else take care of it for you. Perhaps you don't mow your own yard or you don't trim your own trees, for example; something simple like that.

In any aspect of life that you can think of, there are undoubtedly people providing that service on a "done for you" basis, profiting by filling a need felt by people who don't want to do it themselves for whatever reason. The reason they don't want to do it isn't important; what matters is that they don't. **There's a gap in many marketplaces that can be filled by offering to do what people don't want to do on their own, but still want done.**

Earlier, I mentioned our "Cash-in-48-Hours" system. We have an advertising service based on what we've now proven that our customers want—and that's where the profits lie in any business. **What matters isn't necessarily what *you* want; it's what *they* want.** We've found that many of our clients would like a hand-up, a little assistance, so we've found it very profitable to offer "done for you" advertising packages and options for them. Suppose you were looking for a way to advertise, and you approached a local ad agency. They could help you get your ads placed and you might say, "I want national exposure," and then they would buy ad space all over the U.S. in various media. Well, we offer that; but we also offer back-end services and management as well.

Let me explain how that works. Let's say you run a big national ad campaign, and you've got this toll-free hotline for all the leads to come in on. What happens when it does really well, and you're flooded with calls? Usually, it's up to you to convert the leads to sales and do all the customer service work; but we offer to do all that for our clients. **In essence, we've become a full-service advertising and management company. A big part of our business, in fact, is helping clients do all these things under one umbrella.** It's been an extremely successful campaign for us. We've struck a chord with our clients and with our broader marketplace, now that we've discovered that they really want these things done for them. Now, could our clients do all of the above on their own? Of course. In fact, some do. They may choose to advertise other ways, for example. But we offer these services so that people can have another option, so they can choose to have us take care of everything for them.

So give some serious thought to "done for you" services in light of some of the things you experience and do on a regular basis. I think you'll start to see more and more ways that "done for you" is offered in the market at large. Consider retirement accounts. You know, you can manage your own retirement fund; you don't need a broker, though you might need some way of getting onto the trading floor. Essentially, you need a firm to buy and sell through, but you can manage that easily enough: There are all kinds of online brokerage firms available. Still, a lot of people like to have someone take care of their accounts for them. Similarly, there are all kinds of things being done in our society at large that illustrate this principle of "done for you" services.

I think you would be remiss if you didn't find a way to incorporate "done for you" into your business model; and I believe that there are enough examples available across all kinds of industries that there's no excuse not to. **No matter what you sell,** no matter who you sell to, there are things you can do for those people that they probably don't want to do themselves, and might not even know *how* to do themselves. If you add "do it for you" services, products, and opportunities to your mix, you'll see your sales and your profits increase as more people look for ways to get out of that work themselves.

Again, for this to work, **you'll first need to show people that you're an expert**—because they want to know they're working with somebody who knows what they're doing, knows what they're talking about, and can back up what they're saying. **These days, one of the easiest ways to establish that proof is to offer an information product—for example, a report or web video—in which you show people what needs to be done and tell them how they could do it themselves.** By doing that, you prove that you're the expert, and then you can offer your service: your easy, no-risk way of doing it for them.

It may seem odd to give them all the knowledge and information they need to do the task, and then expect them to take you up on the offer; but many people will do just that. Admittedly, some people won't; when Chris was dealing with his electrical outlet problem, he went online and watched a little video of someone else changing theirs out on the free website Ehow.com, and now he feels pretty confident that he can do it on his own and save the electrician's fee. But he also tells me that there are plenty of times when he's watched a video on how to do something, and then decided to hire somebody else to do it for him anyway—because he felt like he just didn't want to tackle it.

So show them how to do it themselves first. Give them that option, and then offer them your service. And consider this: **because you're doing it for them, you can charge a premium**

price, which is one reason "done for you" can be a huge boost to your business model. In this fast-changing world, we're looking for people we can trust, people we can depend on; and once we find somebody like that, why would we want to do a task ourselves? **Just prove to people that you're trustworthy and that you can do what you say, and you can make a fortune by taking care of everything for them.**

POWERFUL
MARKETING IDEA
#11

How to SEPARATE YOURSELF from All of Your Competitors!

You Must Create "Exclusivity."

The single, most important secret that has made us more money than all other factors combined is simply this: **you must create what we call "Exclusivity." There's got to be something that separates you and your company, and all the products and services that you sell, from all your competitors.** And not only do you have to be different, but you have to be different in ways that are very important to the people you're trying to attract as customers—at least in the minds of those prospects.

Now, a lot of people might say, "Oh, there's nothing different about me. There's nothing different about my products and my services... at least, nothing different enough that it's going to cause people to really pay attention to my business." And you're right: there really *is* nothing that much different about your business, which is why **it's up to you to create and build that exclusivity, to differentiate yourself from the crowd.**

I own a book called *Differentiate or Die!* I love that title, because **good marketing is all about separating yourself from everybody else. Some people call what differentiates you from everyone else your Unique Selling Position or a Unique Selling Proposition; a USP, either way.** A USP is critical for any business, not least because there are just too many choices available in the marketplace these days. There are too many decisions for the average consumer to make, too many messages to process. And there are too many "me too" companies. There's a line from a Jackson Brown song that goes, "You take Sally and I'll take Sue, there's really no difference between the two..." Well, there's no real difference between a lot of these companies out there; there's no difference between the products and services they offer. And if there *is* a difference, it's not enough of a difference to really matter.

Plus, you've got all these marketers shouting all at once. There's more competition than ever before. The markets are overcrowded... and that's not a negative thing. In fact, I believe it's a very positive thing. It creates a lot of confusion and frustration, of course, and people tend to suffer from what I call information overload; this is a growing trend where, more than ever, people just feel as if they have more than they can handle. In some ways, that's a problem. **But if you have a strong enough USP, a strong enough way to differentiate yourself from everybody else, you'll solve that problem in their minds—and they'll choose you and your products over all the other choices.** That's the benefit a USP offers.

Let me tell you a story to help you understand the power of all of this. Chris and I were working with one of our clients this morning. We spent over an hour on the telephone with him; we're looking at a joint venture situation, and we're helping him with some marketing ideas. The reason why we're so excited about doing business with this gentleman is because he has one powerful, dramatic story to tell! Nine years ago he had colon cancer, and the doctors gave him six months to live. He was on 32 different medications. His pain was so intense that at one time, he was contemplating suicide. And then he discovered an amazing company out of England that had developed some powerful but little-known nutritional supplements. **Once he started taking them, he slowly got off all 32 of his prescribed medications. He hasn't been sick a single day since, except for an occasional sniffle here or there.** He has more energy than ever before. He's 65 years old and just has a *boundless* energy. He gets up at 6 A.M. every morning and he goes to bed at midnight every night—and it's all because of this nutritional product line that this doctor in England discovered. What an absolutely powerful story! What a way to separate yourself from everybody else and get people's attention!

I'd asked him a few days before if he had any marketing materials, so in the course of our conversation he read us some of the sales copy he'd written. It wasn't bad copy at all; in fact, I think a lot of it is useful. But the thing is, he would have used that material as his lead-in, when really, his lead-in should be *him*. **It's his story that separates him from everybody else. That's what gives him that differentiation he needs, that "exclusivity" I've talked about.** The doctors said he was going to die; they gave him six months to live. He was so depressed, and in so much pain, that he was contemplating suicide. He was on 32 different medications. Then he discovered this amazing product out of England, and it's been a miracle for him. **The cancer is absolutely gone now, and he's in perfect health.** *That* **should be his USP.** All that copy he read to us is all secondary.

So, why don't people do more of this? **First of all, they don't realize how necessary it is.** I've already pointed out that the market is absolutely saturated... and again, that's not a negative thing. That shouldn't be an excuse for you to pull back. **It's an opportunity, because the marketers who stand out tend to grab people's attention and get them interested.** They personalize and humanize the marketplace; and when that's done well, it can make you millions of dollars. **The second reason people don't do this is because they're afraid to.** The fear always pulls them back. It keeps them from sticking their necks out, from getting personal, from using their pictures and telling their stories more, and letting people know these things about themselves.

Look: **people want to do business with people they have something in common with, or whom they feel they can get to know a little.** So you've got to tell them your story. **They want to do business with people they trust, people they believe can really help them—people who understand the pain or suffering they're going through.**

Our new joint venture partner in Georgia has a tremendous story. **People will read his story and identify with all the frustration he went through as the doctors put him on one medication after another.** He was still sick, and he was still in pain, and all the doctors wanted to do was continue to drug him and cut him. They wanted to nuke him to try to kill the cancer. Instead, he found a doctor in England who healed him. **This story sets him up to not only get people's attention and interest, but to build that strong connection with them.**

This single marketing secret has generated a fortune for our company. **From the very beginning, we told our customers our story. We got personal with them.** We told them about all the things we went through—the problems, the frustrations, the headaches, the hassles—the same kinds of struggles we knew our customers were going through. We told them our story so they could identify with us, so they knew that we'd been where they were. **Commonality is a big thing here. It has really built our company, because the commonalities we share with our customers let them know we're real people.** By contrast, too many entrepreneurs don't even use their real names, don't use their pictures, don't tell their stories, don't do anything to create that bond with their customers. But that's what we've done. It's opened the door to long-term relationships with customers who continue to buy from us again and again. It's personalized us. It's made us human. It's separated us from all those nameless, faceless, and personality-less companies out there.

You need to take this page out of our playbook and add it to your own. Don't be afraid to tell dramatic stories, so that you can find some commonality with the people in your marketplace. Build that exclusivity into your whole company. **Because you see, there's nothing much different about you until you put it out there!** This is just so important: you can't let the fear hold you back. People want to do business with other people they feel they know and trust, people who understand their pain. Show them that this is the case. This can really generate a lot of money for you.

One more story: I have a good friend (I've known him for over half my life), and about a year ago we started doing some joint venturing together. We've tested several different offers to my customer base, using him as the front person—his picture, his name. Somewhere in the body copy, it did mention that he's my business partner, and so there was that connection with me. We've tested three different offers now, and let's just say that the response has been less than encouraging. I've been struggling with this, because I know that the models we've been using are proven models that have worked for our company. In other words, I just pulled up sales letters I knew had made money for us and redid them a little for this joint venture; so I knew there was nothing wrong with the sales material. Plus, I knew the list was good, and the offer was good and proven; and I've known all along that the numbers should have been higher. **But there's one thing that I now see as a huge mistake... and that's the fact that I was putting my friend as the front person. They don't know him.**

They don't know his name. They don't trust him.

A lot of our business is built on that kind of trust. Some people think that because they've got an Internet, mail order, or direct response business, somehow that business is different from every other business. But it's not. It's no different than if you had a brick-and-mortar store, and people were coming in and you were greeting them at the door. **It's all about relationships, and building those relationships—and you build them by establishing a unique selling position and creating that exclusivity that separates you from everybody else.** So don't be afraid to do it! It's an important aspect of your entire business model, and if you get it wrong, you'll fail. Without some level of exclusivity, you're going to miss out on business that could be yours. There absolutely has to be something that instantly separates your company from all the other businesses selling similar things.

Often people think, "Well, if I can just invent a widget, then I've got exclusivity. I'll be the only one selling my widget, and if you want it, you've got to get it from me." But the reality is that as soon as you invent a widget, all kinds of other "me too" widgets will pop up that essentially solve the same problem or provide the same benefits to the marketplace. So you've got to do something else.

Consider Apple Computers and their iPod. As amazing as it is, it seems like the iPod has been around for decades. But the first iPod came on the scene in 2001. Now, clear back in 1981, a gentleman in the U.K. filed a patent for a plastic music box. Hmm... plastic music box? Well, that kinda sounds like an iPod! So while Apple came out with their iPods just a decade ago, the concept has been around for a lot longer than that. In fact, there were MP3 players before the iPod, but they were very limited—they could hold maybe 30 songs, at most. **The iPod's ability to hold thousands differentiated that product immediately, and almost destroyed the market for other music players.**

Today, the music scene is full of all kinds of iPod-like devices; and today's iPods do more than just music. They play movies and TV shows and support all kinds of apps. **But the concept for the iPod is nothing new, and wasn't even in 2001.** The iPod itself isn't much different from all the other plastic music boxes that have appeared over the years. **So what makes Apple so successful? Among other things, they developed exclusivity associated with the iPod.** They have a proprietary music file format, though the iPod can play other music files. They have the iTunes software that helps you organize and download your songs to the iPod. They offer the online iTunes Store where you can buy all kinds of products. **The iTunes Store is their proprietary way of delivering content to those iPods; and those files will play only on the iPod and related products.**

So, let's say I have an iPod or an iPhone, and I want to download some great new music. I go to the iTunes Store, I pick some music, I buy it, I put it on my computer, and I sync it up with my device. If I want the latest new movie releases, I can do the same thing. They offer movies, music, TV shows, podcasts, and even a whole section of free educational materials. **All kinds of resources are available there in one store, and you can get access to it all... if you own an iPod, iPad, or iPhone.** Some of it's free content and some of it's pay content, but it's all collected there in one handy, useful store.

By itself, the iPod may not work so well, especially now that other manufacturers have caught up with the technology. It's just another in a long line of plastic music boxes. **But you put it with the proprietary iTunes Store and software, and you've got that necessary exclusivity that differentiates the product.** The iTunes products work hand-in-hand with their iPods, and makes the iPod all the more valuable; and iTunes' exclusivity helps Apple sell more iPods. The reason they sell the hardware is to give them something to put software on. **It was iTunes that made them exclusive—that gave them what they needed to separate themselves from all the manufacturers who sell similar products.**

In this day and age, if you manufacture pretty much anything in the U.S, the second you get it on the shelves there's a factory in China reverse engineering it, figuring out how to make one that's exactly the same but with another brand name on it. **So the idea that you could create something that would have exclusivity simply from the fact that it exists is a pipedream. It's too easy to knock-off your product.** It's too easy to come up with all kinds of other products that are similar. So what do you do then?

In Apple's case, they created iTunes. Now, something like that is beyond the capability of most of us information marketers and similar small entrepreneurs. **We have our names, we have our stories, and we have our brands to make us unique, as opposed to just the products and services we sell.** That's a 100% guaranteed way to do something different and to *be* something different in your marketplace. No matter what you sell, there's only one you. People can get your personality, your uniqueness, only from you. **The more you can set yourself apart in your marketplace, the more you can give yourself exclusivity—that creative edge your marketplace is looking for when they choose who to do business with.**

One of the most "out there," wild characters I can recall was this fellow I used to see on TV who wore a suit coat covered with question marks. Do you remember the guy? His name was Matthew Lesko, and he sold a package of information on how to get government money for anything: to start a business, to go to college, whatever. That was totally a personality-driven business, as far as I was concerned. Anybody can get on the Internet or do some library research and get information on how to apply for government grants, but **Matthew Lesko made a profitable business of it, because he collected it in one place and made things easy for people—and he put a personality behind it.**

He was pretty lively, and he created a persona that made you want to do business with him. He had a real tough job, too, given that you could find all this information on your own, for free, if you just worked at it. But it required a lot of legwork, which was one of the selling points of the product. Instead of busting your hump collecting this information, you could just buy his book. And he used his unique personality to drive those sales. He still does, actually, except that he's mostly moved to the Internet.

There are lots of similar situations out there. For example, there's a car dealership in our town that works that way—in fact, a lot of car dealerships do. Their commercials are personality-driven. There's a huge dealership in Wichita where one of the partners in the company acts as the personality behind the dealership, and he's on all the commercials. Any time you see him on TV, it's him portraying the company and it's his personality that's driving it.

I think the lesson here is that it's difficult to make yourself unique if all you're doing is trying to make your product stand out. It's possible, but it's hard. It's too easy for other people to replicate what you've done with your product or service, and it's too easy for the prospects, who have all these other options to choose from, to do business with someone else because you haven't differentiated yourself enough.

Right now, Chris Lakey happens to be in the market for a cheap car he can drive back and forth to work. He's looking for something as much as 20 years old—but it has to be a luxury car that still has some life in it. So he's been looking at old BMWs, Lexuses, Acuras, Mercedes-Benzes; something he can pick up for a few thousand bucks, but might have fun tinkering with, and have fun driving the 20 miles back and forth to the office every day. He's looking all over the U.S. to find a car that fits what he's looking for. He has an idea of what he wants, and it's pretty specific. Well, he could go to any dealer if he wanted to pick up a car and say, "I'm not really that picky. I just want a BMW," or whatever the case may be. If he were buying new, he'd probably do that, and he could buy the same model from any BMW dealer. There's no real reason to choose one over the other, at least not on the basis of the cars themselves.

Now, some dealerships do offer better service than others, and some are closer to Chris's home than others. Maybe some are located in the county instead of in the city, so the tax rate is cheaper. There are all kinds of factors to take into account when choosing to buy a car, other than just the fact that you need *this* particular car. So those dealers have to compete for the business based not on the specs of the vehicle, but on what they can do for Chris as he's looking to buy a car from them. **The point is that in almost every kind of business, the personality of the owner or the entrepreneur behind it is going to be largely responsible for whether you have this**

feature of exclusivity or not.

So think about your business model, what you sell, and who you sell to. If people can get the product you sell—or something similar that does the same thing or promises the same benefits—from somebody else, then all you have left is the other things you can offer: like your personality, who you are, what you bring to the table, and what you can provide for them. Those kinds of things will determine whether you get more business or not. **So create exclusivity, and offer that "something different" that becomes a vital part of your business and who you are, setting you apart from all your competitors.**

Competition is only going to get worse in the future, not better—but that doesn't have to be bad news for you. In fact, it can actually be *good* news, because the customers these days are more confused and frustrated than ever. **If you can do things to separate yourself from the crowd, at least in ways that are important to your prospects, your marketing message will cut like a knife through all the noise out there.**

POWERFUL MARKETING IDEA
#12

The Type of Offer That Buyers Can't Resist!

Everyone Loves
an Exclusive Offer!

Exclusive offers are very attractive to the average consumer. In fact, **the more a prospect perceives that your offer has been designed with them *specifically* in mind, the more they're going to want it.** Which leads us to a corollary: the things that people want the most are the things that other people can't get. In other words, the more they feel that an offer's intended for just anybody, the less they're likely to want it.

Therefore, **you always have to build something unique into whatever you're selling, in order to draw people in.** The hard part here is that there's nothing that's particularly unique anymore... and there hasn't been, really, for thousands of years. As the Bible puts it, "There's nothing new under the sun." That's part of the Old Testament, so someone pointed that out well before the arrival of Christ himself. Despite this fact—or, perhaps, because of it—**everybody in every marketplace *wants* something new and special.** So if you want to make money with your offers, you have to make your best effort to create such things, so you can differentiate what you're offering from all the similar offers out there.

The best examples of what I would call exclusive offers—products that fit like a hand to a glove, so that when people get one they say, "This was designed for me"—are our websites. We've sold millions of dollars worth of "beta tester" promotions since we started developing websites back in the mid-1990s, when the Internet was first taking off. Back then, people might pay $20,000-30,000 for something you can get now for less than $1,000—and often for less than $500. Well, we were one of the very first development companies to offer inexpensive websites to the average consumer. We've specialized in what we call "beta tester" offers, which is where we release a group of websites to testers because they're not quite ready for the marketplace yet—there's always something new that has to be checked out. But we don't release them for free; **we simply give our customers a very special deal on a block of websites.** They're happy because they got them for a low price, and we're happy because we made some money *and* got the bugs worked out of our websites during the testing process.

For example: for many years, we sold different versions of a block of 300 websites to our customers. We were always revising them, making them better, trying new features, and the like. **We'd give our customers 50 of those websites for a phenomenally low price, making it clear that they were getting this deal because these were beta versions that hadn't been tested fully.** We'd tell them we needed beta testers to help us get the bugs out of them—and then we would deliver the sites to them and just blow them away! They would be shocked when they saw what we'd given them; **the quality was high, and the price was a bargain.** Oftentimes we'd throw in a few years of free hosting, too—and all for as little as $9 for all 50 sites, though the price was more likely to be $29 or $39.

No sooner did they get those sites than we'd follow-up with a special offer, just for them, for an additional block of 250 websites that were similar to the 50 they'd purchased. Our offer pointed out, "Look, you're already a beta tester for our first 50 websites...", and we thanked them profusely. They had a chance to go on the Internet and look over their sites, so we demonstrated to them that we were trustworthy. In all these ways, we proved that our offer was everything that we said it was. They were already sold on the concept of being beta testers for these first 50 websites, so we knew that this custom-tailored offer for an additional 250 websites was the perfect upsell.

This was a true "hand in glove" offer. Now, think about that; because that's how it has to work. Visualize a glove that your hand fits into perfectly. It's wintertime as I'm writing this, and it's very, very cold here. Most of us who live here don't mind the cold weather…as long as we're dressed for it. So we all wear gloves whenever we go outside. Think about how a nice, well-fitting glove feels, and how warm it keeps your hands. Think of how warm a prospect feels when they fit perfectly into an offer—when it feels like it's been tailored especially for them.

Our beta tester offer was custom-designed just for our existing customers, and it gave them more of what they'd already bought from us. We knew that they were already sold, and it let us speak to that group in a way that let them *know* that the offer was just for them. We've done that with other types of offers, where we try to give our prospects a small piece of the much bigger piece that we want to sell them later. With our websites, that's easy to do.

In the next few months, we're going to be developing a new offer where we give our beta testers 100 websites to start with, and then we're going to follow up with an offer for an additional 1,000—or maybe even more. We might even start out by giving them 240 websites, and then offer them 2,400 more. **Those kinds of deals just blow people away, because those deals speak directly to what the customers want.** It gives them more of what they already had, and it's exclusive for them.

And remember, the second part of this strategy is that the things people want the most are the things that others can't get. As I write this, we're putting together copy for a new seminar that's coming up in the next month. Over this past weekend, I decided to limit the seminar to just 73 people, each of whom can bring a guest of their choice. Now, why did I do that? Because it made the product super-exclusive. They know that if they're the 74th person to try to sign up, they're not going to get in. It's special—and that's what people really want.

You know, in some ways people are very, very complex; and the smarter they are, the more complicated they are. But in other ways (especially from an emotional standpoint), people are very simple. **Once of the simplicities within the complexity of human behavior is the fact that we all want what other people can't have.** We all want things that are special, created just for us. We all want to feel important; in fact, many of us are *desperate* to feel important. These days, most people don't; they just feel like numbers, or walking wallets. The more you can do to show them how much you appreciate them, that you want to give them access to something very limited, something that other people can't get—the better they'll respond.

We've got another extremely limited offer going at the moment that has a very firm cut-off point. If a prospect misses out on it, then someone else is going to take their position; we're very clear that there are only so many of these positions available. **In a situation like this one, people fight to get in, so they can lock themselves in and not have to worry about somebody else coming along and grabbing that exclusive offer.** That being the case, the profit potential for an offer like this is immense.

These things don't just happen by accident: you have to work to make them special. So how do you accomplish this? By becoming intimately aware of every aspect of the marketplace. As I've emphasized repeatedly in this book, **you must put yourself in the shoes of the people you're trying to reach, and learn every detail you can about them.** What's most important to them? What conversations are going on in their heads, right this moment? How can you strongly communicate your offer in such a way as to make it more desirable?

I just got an email from a man I spent some time with last summer, during our Branson Seminar in Branson, Missouri. He and I had talked about an idea for making millions of dollars back then, and now, months later, he's emailing me with some information on this offer. I've read his email five times—and I still don't understand what the hell he's talking about. He rambled on for three pages and didn't tell me a single thing. He didn't make the offer attractive or exclusive one bit. If it weren't for the fact that I really care about this man, I wouldn't have paid any attention to the offer at all—I would have scrapped it in a second. But instead I'm trying to work with him, trying to go back and forth with him to understand what he's trying to say.

Your offers can't be like that. They have to be crystal clear, so your prospects can instantly see the advantages you've set up for them. **They've got to immediately grasp just how perfect your offer is for them—to perceive, just from looking, that it will fit them like a glove.** To achieve this kind of transparency, you must develop and maintain an intimate awareness of the people you're trying to reach. Learn what's most important to them, and how you can clearly (and I do mean *clearly*) communicate the most important benefits in the shortest period of time, so that they'll instantly see your offer for what it is and will instantly be attracted to it.

It really is amazing how human psychology dominates this equation—how much it feeds into developing effective sales tactics. **You're fighting the tide if you fail to take into account the psychological aspects of business;** the cold math isn't all you need to help you sell your products and opportunities. The exclusivity factor really weighs heavily here, and you can see this when you look at real life examples of how people go about their daily lives and exercise their spending habits. Consider how people respond to any Limited Edition of just about anything. **If they know that only a certain number of a product was made, then all of a sudden the value goes up.** Think of an art print that an artist created only a few hundred copies of; that alone can cause the value to soar. Now, suppose he signed and numbered a select handful of those items. If you have one of those, then your piece of art is even more valuable—simply because there are very few of them available. This kind of exclusivity is what makes most unique art pieces worth more than generic, copied pieces.

When Chris Lakey was a kid, he used to collect baseball and basketball cards. You know, it's one thing just to open a pack of cards, and know that the cards inside are also owned by kids all over the U.S., and that a particular card you're holding is worth a few pennies because it's the same as millions of other cards out there. But usually, some of the cards are available only in limited editions—and you might get lucky. The card company will print on the card pack the odds of what you might pull out of a particular pack of cards. It might be that one out of every 100,000 packs contains an autographed card by whoever happens to be the hottest person in the sport. Chris remembers specifically that back in the early 1990s, Shaquille O'Neal was the hot basketball rookie—and so it was a real thrill to pull a Limited Edition Shaquille O'Neal card. Kids would open dozens of packs of cards trying to get one.

Well, why would you care about any Limited Edition card? **Because it's exclusive.** If you have one, it's likely that no one else you know has one. Chris remembers pulling one of the Limited Edition Shaquille O'Neal cards from a pack once, when he was 15 or 16 years old —and although it wasn't signed, it was worth about $120 at the time. It was just a piece of heavy paper with a picture of a basketball player on it, but the fact that there were only so many of them to go around and *he had one* made him value it more than any old sports card.

His 13-year-old son still has that card stashed somewhere in his room, sealed in a big, heavy piece of protective hard plastic. It's worth ten bucks or so now. But Chris is hoping that one day, that card will become worth something again, and maybe his son can sell it for a little bit of money at some point... or just keep it for the novelty's sake. The point here is that back when it was new, Chris really wanted that card; he wanted all the cards like that. He spent a lot of time and money acquiring meaningless packs of cards to try to find that one Limited Edition card that he knew he wanted the most—**because if he got it, then other people didn't have it. That's the way people are with all kinds of things.**

Similarly, some people like to drive Limited Edition sports cars. If it happens that the manufacturer made only 1,000 of that particular auto, then they're willing to spend more to acquire one. You probably have examples in your own life where you're like that for one thing or another. In our areas of interest or need, we love to get exclusive offers—offers that we perceive are available only to us, or at least to only a few people. **We look for deals that aren't available just anywhere.** We rummage through garage sales looking for that perfect find… that one thing you jump on because no one else can get it, and here it is right in front of you! Let's say you go to the Salvation Army Thrift Store, and you find something they somehow mispriced—something that should have been sold for more. Suddenly, you've scored a good deal on something that isn't available to anybody else—and that makes you feel really good, doesn't it?

That's how your prospects feel when you present them with a perfect fit that you offer for a compelling price. **And it doesn't necessarily have to be a specific item; it could be something more general that lets them know how much you appreciate doing business with them.** Recently, Chris tells me, he received an email from a big electronics chain that said they were having a special after-hours event, and he was invited. Apparently the ad wasn't compelling enough to get him out of his home to drive that half-hour to where the store was located, because he didn't go; but the point is, they *did* extend the invitation to this exclusive event for their "preferred customers." They wanted him to feel special. Now, no doubt they were thronged with people who brought in that little slip from the email that was their ticket to attend the after-hours event... so they could spend money with the store that had made them feel special. In a sense, they all had Golden Tickets that let them get better deals on some items they wanted anyway; and having been made to feel special, do you suppose those people will return and spend more money? Of course they will.

We all want to feel special like that; **so as a marketer, you need to find a way to give your customers and prospects that feeling, so they can appreciate being on the inside.** Nobody wants something that's readily available. Have you ever seen someone wearing a ring with a stone made of coal or sand?

Probably not. Nobody wants a sand ring; they want a diamond ring. Why? Because diamonds are rare, and therefore in demand. The cost is high, and a diamond ring is much more exclusive than any plain ring; so people want one. And they don't want just any diamond either, or they would be more likely to accept the inexpensive synthetic ones. No, people want the best natural diamonds possible, diamonds of a high grade, especially those that are naturally colored; those are especially scarce. In other words, people prefer the stones that are genuinely rare, of extraordinarily limited availability.

Exclusive things make people feel good, which is why you have to carefully evaluate precisely what your customers really, really want the most—and then give it a twist that makes it even more special. What do they feel would be an exclusive buy for them? What do they feel would put them on the inside, put them in the know, or to put them in a position where they can get something that no one else can get? Maybe that's a limited time offer, available to a small group of people, like the one I mentioned earlier. Maybe you find another way to pull out the stops for a preferred group of customers. The point is, you've *got* to come up with that angle that everybody wants, but only a handful can get. People will pay big money for exclusivity; so when you add it to your offers, you'll see your sales will increase.

And one of the things you can do when you're positioning yourself like this is to use what information you have to your advantage. Let's say you know that 10% of your customers are likely to take advantage of your offer, and you have 100 customers (just to have a round number to simplify the math). Well, why not tighten up that offer and make it exclusive to only the first 10 people who respond? Just come right out and say it in your sales copy — and be sure to stick to that number like glue, so you have credibility on your side the next time you do it. **I guarantee that people will respond to that promise of exclusivity.** Set the number wherever you're comfortable. You might even bump it up to 12 or 15, but cut it off when you get there; otherwise, what is your exclusivity worth? **If you're worried about the fact that making something exclusive will limit your profits, then juice up the value some and raise the price.**

And in any case, you'll probably have a lot more than 100 customers to offer something to. For example, we'll often invite all of them to do business with us or get involved in a new opportunity, a new project, or a new service. **So we're dealing with large numbers; and if in fact only 10% of our customers got involved with us on a particular project, that would be 1,500 people.** Even if we said we were looking for only 200, 300, or 500 people to get involved in something, while that would be a small percentage of our entire group of preferred customers, it's still a lot of people.

The number depends on your model — on what you're looking to accomplish. **But keep in mind that the number needs to be real.** If it's not, if you don't fulfill on your promises or it's obvious that you don't mean what you say, people will figure it out and you'll lose your credibility. **There's no real exclusivity if you say "this offer is only for *this* number of people," and it turns out that it's not.** So make it legit, based on your own numbers and your profit needs. Arrange things so that if you make the offer exclusive to 20 customers, you'll make more money in a week than you've made the entire month before. While you don't need to tell them that, you can't be shy about the number of people involved.

Make sure that they know how exclusive the offer truly is. When played right, this principal works wonderfully well—because it provides you with a psychological edge that most people simply can't resists. You've made them feel like they've won when they grab that offer, like they've pulled one over on you and their friends and all the other poor slobs who didn't make it in... which means that you win, too. In the end, this can also give you the edge you need to do more business with them.

The important thing to know is that you control the perceptions here, to a large degree—assuming they believe you, or know that they can trust you. You're the one who builds the value; you're the one who builds the exclusivity into your offers, making them more unique, more special, and seemingly less available to everybody else.

Start paying attention to how other marketers are doing this, because it doesn't just happen by accident. You can't just throw crap together and hope people will figure it out, like the guy did who sent me that impenetrable email this morning. As Nathaniel Hawthorne once said, "Easy reading is damn hard writing." **In other words, the more you work on it, the clearer it becomes.** So work hard on your copywriting, and do everything you can to build your offers so that you make your prospects feel special. That's surprisingly rare, as logical as it may seem; **very few marketers bother to make their prospects feel special.**

If you can do that effectively, you'll grab all the customers your competitors aren't getting—and you'll practically mint money.

FREE Bonus Book!

50 IN 50.

BY **T.J. ROHLEDER**
AKA AMERICA'S
BLUE JEAN MILLIONAIRE

"<u>50</u> of the Greatest Things
Learned in My First <u>50</u> Years
of Life and How They May
Be Vital to Your Success."

Dear Friend,

This small book contains 100 of the very best ideas I have ever learned about success and money. I hope you enjoy and prosper greatly from them.

To celebrate my 50th birthday, I thought it would be a fun idea to put together a list of my 50 greatest money-making secrets I have learned in my first 50 years of life! Well... I couldn't stop at 50 secrets. Besides, one of the greatest secrets I've learned is to always strive to give people more!

So, in the spirit of giving more – and to celebrate my 50th birthday by giving you more – I offer these 100 powerful ideas to you. **ENJOY!**

Sincerely,

T.J. Rohleder
www.TJRohleder.com

There are only 3 ways to build a business:

1. Get more customers.

2. Sell more high-ticket items – for bigger profits.

3. Sell more often to your customers!

Almost all million-dollar marketing ideas are transferable from one business to another.

---

50 IN 50.

Selling is the art of proving that what you have to offer is worth far, far MORE than the money they must give up.

50 IN 50.

CREATE *IRRESISTABLE* OFFERS!

"I want to create offers that are like heads of fresh lettuce that are thrown into a pen of starving rabbits!"

(I wrote this in 1997.)

50 IN 50.

Think on paper!

The very act of putting your ideas on paper forces you to think!

50 IN 50.

* * * * *

Blur the lines between your work and play.

* * * * *

50 IN 50.

The power of the 5 A.M. Club:

- Force yourself to get out of bed before you want to – and put on a big pot of strong black coffee. – Pull out some paper and pens and start writing!

- Ideas <u>will</u> come to you and through you – that you would <u>never</u> have discovered <u>if</u> you stayed in bed!

There is a magic at work here that's hard to explain! You must experience it – <u>before</u>

50 IN 50.

Less is more.

It's far better to be a
master at 2 or 3 things –
than to be average at doing
a whole bunch of things.

50 IN 50.

* * *

The real business
is between our ears
and in our hearts –
not in the office!

* * *

50 IN 50.

$ $ $

A strong <u>risk-reversal offer</u> takes a lot of courage, but this can make you **<u>super rich</u>**!

$ $ $

50 IN 50.

"I have a lot of competition, but <u>ZERO</u> competitors!"

Kerry Thomas

50 IN 50.

$ $ $ $ $

Test new ideas…
but <u>never</u> stray too
far away from the
winning formulas
that have been
proven to be the
most successful in
your marketplace.

$ $ $ $ $

50 IN 50.

* * * * *

**All this talk about
retirement is nonsense!
Work gives our lives
purpose, meaning, and
structure. Stop telling me
to take it easy...** *I'll have
eternity to take it easy!*

* * * * *

50 IN 50.

The question all marketers
<u>must</u> constantly ask:

What's next?

50 IN 50.

Jump – and the net will appear!

- √ Make the commitment first.
- √ Set the deadline!
- √ Run the ad – then scramble to put the fulfillment together!
- √ Make <u>BIG</u> <u>PROMISES</u> to groups of customers – and then scramble to make them real!
- √ Do whatever you can to force yourself to do more!

50 IN 50.

**Salespeople get paid
to hear the word
"no!"**

**A "no" does not
mean "no" to the
aggressive person
who wants the sale!**

50 IN 50.

• • • • •

**Take good care of
the people who take
good care of you!**

• • • • •

50 IN 50.

> **Your best work
> is still out there!**

50 IN 50.

Better to strengthen your back than to lighten your load!

50 IN 50.

All growth comes from
consciously living outside
of your comfort zone.

If you're not doing things
on a regular basis that scare
you just a little (or a lot!)
– you're not growing.

50 IN 50.

More business problems are created by indecision than bad decision.

Go ahead and take massive action! Try many different things and fail and learn from all your mistakes while daring big and failing again and again!

50 IN 50.

Spend <u>more</u> money – to close more sales!

1. You can't go wrong if you are spending this money on super qualified prospects.
2. You are selling big ticket items with good margins.

In some cases (as long as your percentage of conversion is going up) you can't spend too much money!

50 IN 50.

Most marketers are weak.

* They quit way too soon.
* They are too worried about offending their prospects or customers.
* Or, they simply don't know that there is a great deal more money laying on the table that could and should be theirs – if they simply went after it more aggressively and then stayed after it until they got it!

50 IN 50.

Your business is like a bicycle. Either you keep it moving or you fall down!

- Keep searching for your next big winner!
- Keep finding better ways to give your customers and prospects what you know they want the most!

50 IN 50.

Create as many
"businesses within
your business" as
you possibly can.

50 IN 50.

Get your *best offer* in front of <u>more people</u> and follow-up like crazy!

50 IN 50.

**The best product
does not always win,
*but the best marketing
always does!***

50 IN 50.

* * * * * * * * *

All business is
show business!

* * * * * * * * *

50 IN 50.

Your best customers are like fires. They go out if unattended.

- The key word is "relationship."

- The better they "feel" about you – the more money they will give you!

- Remember, the fire never dies as long as you keep feeding it!

50 IN 50.

Many people think nothing of spending $60,000.00 to put their teenage son or daughter in college for 4 to 6 years so they can become a nameless, faceless middle managers and make enough money to drive a nice car and live in an upper-middle class neighborhood.

Those same people will totally freak out when asked to cough up $3,000.00 for a marketing seminar that is designed to show them how to make millions of dollars.

Why is this?

50 IN 50.

"What are you willing to do?"

The answer to these six words will determine how much money you will ultimately make.

50 IN 50.

* * * * * * * * * *

Rock star or brain surgeon?

Your time is the most precious commodity you have. *So why would you want to sell it for any amount of money?* <u>Don't</u> <u>do</u> <u>this</u>! Find as many ways as you can to make money that have little or even nothing to do with the amount of time you put into it.

* * * * * * * * * *

50 IN 50.

What is the best way to deepen your relationship with your customers?

> The answer: hold seminars, tele-seminars, workshops, and other "training" events that bond with them by showing them that you care and really want to help them.

> You can also do this through the careful creation of all kinds of information products that are sold or sent to them.

50 IN 50.

The only 3 ways to make money:

1. <u>Sell your time for money</u>. You charge by the hour and trade your life for a paycheck.

2. <u>Sell a product or service</u>. Your money comes from the sale of the gizmo – not the time or work it takes to sell it.

3. <u>Passive income</u>. Your money makes you more money <u>without</u> your direct effort. All of the world's richest people make their money with the third method. Their money comes to them automatically from a wide variety of cash-producing investments. Their money keeps making them more money! Do everything you can to make as much of your money as possible in the third area! What would you rather be: A rock star or a brain surgeon?

50 IN 50.

The 9 Major Marketing Mistakes
and How to Avoid Them!

1. **No Focus:** The list of prospects is #1. Hone in on one specific highly qualified prospect. Know them in the most intimate way.

2. **No Compelling Offer:** You must have something hot to get people to take action now!

3. **No Deadline:** The more urgency you can build into your offer – the higher your response rate will be!

4. **No Testimonials:** What other people say about you is much more important than what you say about yourself.

5. **No Measurement of Results:** The only thing that counts is ROI (Return on Investment). Know your numbers! Don't get hung up on response rates.

6. **No Follow-Up:** Most people are giving up on 'em way too soon. Eighty-two percent of sales happen after the first follow-up!

7. **Trying to Be Cute and Funny:** Use direct response (not "Madison Avenue") advertising.

8. **BAD Copy:** The right words rule!

9. **Too Much Reliance on One Media:** Diversify! Multiple legs on table!

50 IN 50.

Here is one of my favorite quotes that is right next to my big clock, so I can see it all the time:

"Business is <u>always</u> a struggle. There are always obstacles and competitors. There is never an open road, except the wide road that leads to failure. Every great success has always been achieved by fight. Every winner has scars. Those who succeed are the efficient few. They are the few who have the ambition and willpower to develop themselves."

Herbert N. Casson

50 IN 50.

Our greatest rock-n-roll role model is the heavy metal band "AC/DC."

"AC/DC" has recorded nearly 20 albums and sold over 200 million albums worldwide with the same 3 chord songs on each one. The fans don't care! In fact, not giving them the same 3 chords in every song on every album would cause them to stop buying! Their worldwide fan base would dry up immediately!

Find your formula and, once you do find it, <u>never</u> <u>stray</u> <u>from</u> <u>it</u>!

50 IN 50.

Hard work is good for your soul.

√ Plus, it may keep you alive longer!

√ And even if it doesn't, it will add more life to your years.

√ "Hard work never killed a man. Men die of boredom, psychological conflict, and disease. Indeed, the harder you work – the happier you will be." *David Oglivy*

√ "Seek above all else a game worth playing and play it as if your entire life and sanity depended on it...for it does!" *Edward DeRopp*

50 IN 50.

More problems = more action!

So bring it on, baby!

You get rich by consistently doing the things other people cannot or will not do. Taking huge risks, putting your neck on the line, and facing the tremendous struggles (from backing yourself into a corner or tackling more than you can handle) is the secret to creating lots of problems – THAT CAN SPUR YOU ON BIG TIME!

50 IN 50.

Delegate your weaknesses.

Focus on
your strengths.

50 IN 50.

The 10 main things that made us millions:

1. We knew the market – <u>before</u> we started our business.

2. Previous business experience.

3. Partnership of two very different people.

4. Fell in love with our business.

5. Focused on serving customers.

6. Help from experts.

7. Help from many others!

8. Learned the art and skill of developing products and offers.

9. Learned how to develop front-end and back-end marketing systems.

10. Strived to give our customers <u>MORE</u> than they received from our competitors.

(From our 10-year anniversary seminar in 1998.)

50 IN 50.

Never Fear Objections.

Don't hide! Be upfront about the skepticism you know they feel… Bring up the biggest objections yourself. Then overcome them one by one. You'll win their trust and respect – and you'll get their money.

The best prospects have major objections that must be faced head-on and not skated around.

50 IN 50.

The pain
of discipline
<u>hurts</u> <u>less</u>
than the pain
of regret.

50 IN 50.

You have to *roll*
with the punches!

Keep getting up –
every time you get
knocked down.

50 IN 50.

Are all highly-successful entrepreneurs a little crazy?

Maybe, but one thing is for certain: almost all of them tend to be very creative. The symptoms of creativity are also directly related to insanity! Check it out for yourself:

CREATIVITY	MADNESS
High energy	Mania, insomnia
Heightened senses	Mood disorder
Eccentricity	Erratic behavior
Emotional expressiveness	Emotional volatility
Spontaneity	Impulsiveness
Risk taking	Recklessness
Single-mindedness	Obsessiveness
Unusual perceptions	Distortions of reality
Visions	Hallucinations
Big ideas	Grandiosity
Fluency of ideas	Flight of ideas
High standards	Perfectionism
Feelings of giftedness	Narcissism

The more you think about this, you'll realize that all great entrepreneurs definitely have all of the symptoms on the left-hand side of this chart!

50 IN 50.

STOP LOWERING YOUR PRICES!

Low prices are reserved for people who <u>cannot</u> market themselves effectively. **If you're competing on price, you haven't established enough value in the minds of your prospective customers.** It's up to you to prove – without a doubt – that the best prospective buyers in your market should be giving more of their money to you. Marketing is all about differentiation, but it's up to you to create those perceptions of difference in the minds of the people you most want on your customer list.

50 IN 50.

Strive to be <u>more</u> "human" in all of your communications.

√ Be real!

√ Be raw!

√ Be imperfect!

Let them feel what you feel and see the REAL person behind the words they are reading.

50 IN 50.

Learn by doing.

You can't let a simple thing like the fact that you've <u>never</u> done something or don't know how to do it stop you from doing it.

The fact that entrepreneurs are willing to boldly step out and face the unknown – and figure it all out as they go – is the one thing that separates them from everyone else.

50 IN 50.

• • • • •

The front-end builds your list, **but the back-end makes you rich!**

• • • • •

50 IN 50.

The #1 reason that the most solid businesses begin to decline is simply because they <u>STOP</u> doing the things that took them to the top.

- They lose their edge.

- They lose their focus.

- They lose their hunger.

- They lose the boldnees and creativity they had when they were struggling their way to the top. They become conservative and complacent. Now they are easy targets for all of the others who are just like they once were!

50 IN 50.

"You <u>can't</u> kill an
elephant with a BB gun!"

Bill Glazer

People are trying to get
HUGE results with a small
amount of effort and expense.

YOU <u>CAN'T</u> DO IT!

50 IN 50.

SPECIAL

BONUS

<u>50</u> SECRETS

50 IN 50.

People are looking for
and willing to spend a
ton of money for:

<u>The</u> <u>Magic</u>
<u>Pill</u>!

This is the product or
service that they
perceive can instantly
and automatically give
them something they
badly want.

50 IN 50.

> **Strive to make your offer
> so attractive, compelling,
> and irresistible *that only
> a lunatic would say "No!"***

50 IN 50.

"What people want is a miracle!"

Gene Swartz
(One of the World's Greatest
Direct Response Marketing
Copywriters of All-Time)

> People want easy answers and quick solutions.

> People love pat answers – easy solutions – simple ideas – and stuff that sounds good! They want sugar coated bullshit! They like words and ideas that are coated with syrup and sprinkled with sugar!

50 IN 50.

The 4 laws of self teaching:

1. *You are your greatest teacher.*
2. You can learn <u>anything</u> you want to learn.
3. You <u>must</u> take total responsibility for everything that happens to you.
4. Experience + Reflection = Wisdom!

50 IN 50.

The great Olympic runner,
Steve Prefontaine said:

"There may be men
who can beat me –
but they'll have to
bleed to do it!"

50 IN 50.

• • • • •

Step out in faith – and figure it out *as you go!*

• • • • •

50 IN 50.

**Do everything
possible to shift
the power and get
<u>them</u> to chase <u>you</u> –
*rather than you
chasing them!***

---

50 IN 50.

P. T. Barnum-ize every offer!

– Big!
– Blow it up!
– Bold!
– Explosive!
– Wow them!
– History making!
– Whiz-bang!
– Hype it!
– Jazz it up!
– Make it rock!

50 IN 50.

Fight like hell, but choose your battles wisely.

50 IN 50.

If the desks are too neat and clean... and the people all look relaxed... **the company is in BIG TROUBLE!!!**

50 IN 50.

$ $ $

Happiness
is...
a never-ending stream
of positive cash-flow!

$ $ $

50 IN 50.

Retirement = **Death.**

50 IN 50.

Failure is the best education.

- Test a lot of different things.
- Set out to try bold things (on a small basis).
- And then never repeat what didn't work!
- The more you test – and fail – the better! Why? Because you will ultimately discover what works best.

50 IN 50.

Stop waiting for inspiration!
Instead, you must get up
every morning with the
determination to press on –
and do creative work – even if
you don't feel like it. Your
motion will create the
emotion.

"Most of life is routine – dull
and grubby – but routine is
the momentum that keeps a
man going. If you wait for
inspiration you'll be standing
on the corner after the parade
is a mile down the street."

Ben Nicholas

50 IN 50.

You serve yourself
best – *when you serve
others the most.*

50 IN 50.

A good swipe file can make you a ton of money!

> Use it to jump-start your thinking.
> Get new creative ideas that you would have never discovered without it.
> It's a brainstorming tool – if you realize that all great selling ideas can be transferred from one product, service, or business to another.
> In other words, the ideas that are or have brought in a ton of money for one person or company can be worth a fortune to you!

50 IN 50.

Sell yourself first. Bond with them. Then sell your stuff!

√ It's so much easier to sell things to people AFTER you make a strong connection with them.

√ You must break down their sales resistance <u>before</u> you start pitching to them.

√ Honest Abe knew this: "If you would win a man to your cause, first convince him that you are his sincere friend."
Abraham Lincoln

50 IN 50.

Formal generalized education sucks!

The only thing that's important is specialized knowledge and experience that is directed in a very specific direction.

50 IN 50.

< < < < < <

**Life, love,
and business
favor the bold!**

> > > > > >

50 IN 50.

• • • • •

Love will find a way – indifference will find an excuse.

√ Learn to love the things you do that bring you the largest number of sales and profits!

√ Love makes all burdens light. This is the key to doing your <u>best</u> work!

• • • • •

50 IN 50.

"The road to excess leads to enlightenment!"

William Blake
(A man who pushed the envelope!)

√ You <u>never</u> know how far you can go until and unless you push yourself way too far!

√ You push it hard – until it breaks – then fix it – then push it even harder, until it breaks again!

√ Whoever said, "Don't bite off more than you can chew," was wrong! The secret to wealth is to constantly be involved in way more projects than you can possibly handle! You must boldly push beyond your limits in order to expand them. The higher you climb, the more you can see… SO KEEP CLIMBING HIGHER!

50 IN 50.

* * * * * * * * * * * * * *

Whoever owns the BIGGEST and MOST RESPONSIVE mailing list is <u>king!</u>

* * * * * * * * * * * * * *

50ɪɴ50.

The **true art** of selling is to make people feel that they are the ones chasing you!

To be very aggressive with your marketing <u>without</u> appearing like you need or even care whether they do business with you.

50 IN 50.

Catch yourself on fire and they will come to watch you burn!

Winston Churchill said it best:

"Before you can inspire with emotion, you must be swamped with it yourself."

50 IN 50.

• • • • • • • • •

Wise men have <u>many</u> doubts.

• • • • • • • • •

50 IN 50.

Database marketing in 3 words:

1. **Segment**

2. **Concentrate**

3. **Dominate!**

50 IN 50.

Never give up!

I read somewhere that...
**"Success is the ability to hold on,
long after others have let go."**

Like many quotes, it sounded good
so I committed it to memory. But
the longer I am self-employed,
the more I know how true this is!

50 IN 50.

The easy way to dramatically increase your persuasive power: <u>WRITE</u> <u>MORE</u>!

> Consistent writing about your #1 subject helps to crystalize your thinking.

> This, in turn, <u>will</u> make you a much more persuasive thinker. You will speak with greater confidence and power. Your ideas will be sharper and more people will want to buy and re-buy from you.

50 IN 50.

Breakdowns can lead to breakthroughs!

√ Adversity is good for your soul. It builds character. It makes you stronger. It shapes you.

√ Adversity is the great developer of all great entrepreneurs.

50 IN 50.

$ $ $

Getting rich <u>and</u>
<u>staying</u> <u>rich</u> are two
entirely different
things.

They require a
different set of skills.

$ $ $

50 IN 50.

If you don't know it can't be done, you can do it.

An educated person will stay up all night and worry about things that most of us never even think about. We are too damn busy doing the deal to worry about anything.

50 IN 50.

Your best will continue to get better!

√ Stay committed to mastery! Stay hungry. Continue to learn all you can. Give each project everything you've got – and your best will continue getting better!

√ The real joy of mastery is when you finally have the ability to do amazing things...in the most natural way. To get to the place where great things seem to flow out of you in the most natural way...where all of the things that were once difficult are now easy, and even fun!

50 IN 50.

> > > > > < < < < <

The <u>why</u> to do something always comes before the <u>how</u> to do it! *This is the secret behind all great achievers.*

Great achievers set the goal – and then figure it out as they go along. You can't let a little thing like not knowing how you're going to do something stop you!

> > > > > < < < < <

50 IN 50.

> **If you think the way you've always thought –** *you'll get everything you've always got!*

50 IN 50.

"Selling is a performance!"

Dan Kennedy

Dan also says that selling <u>is</u> <u>not</u> <u>serving</u>. The root word for serving is "servant." Serving your customer is a vital role in the marketing and customer service area of your business – but not the "selling" side of what you do. Selling is all about control and power over the prospect or customer. You are the one in charge, not them. You are the one who leads them to buy. You must be the one who controls the entire selling process, not them.

50 IN 50.

The 10 most powerful
two-letter words in
the English language:

**If it is to be
it is <u>up</u> <u>to</u> <u>me</u>.**

50 IN 50.

. . . . .

**Remain
open,
flexible,
and curious.**

. . . . .

50 IN 50.

Customers go where
they are invited –
and stay where they
are appreciated.

50 IN 50.

$ $ $ $ $

The door will
<u>always</u> be open to
the person who can
make money for others.

$ $ $ $ $

50 IN 50.

- - - - - - - -

There's an easy way and a hard way to do something.

Only a fool chooses the hard way just for the sake of doing it hard. The smart person strives to keep it as easy – simple – and manageable as possible.

- - - - - - - -

50 IN 50.

— $ $ $ —

Relationship Marketing:

Win their hearts – then win their pocketbooks!

— $ $ $ —

50 IN 50.

* * * * *

Always have your next project waiting in the wings!

* * * * *

50 IN 50.

Problems contain massive
amounts of energy. The
same problems that kill some
people – cause others to
shoot straight to the top!

The pressure from the
problems should be used to
create the solutions!

50 IN 50.

Many people are <u>too smart</u> to get rich. Their intelligence is a trap. They use all their mental powers to find and focus on all the obstacles – rather than the outcomes.

50 IN 50.

If you always think the way you always thought... <u>you'll</u> <u>always</u> <u>get</u> <u>what</u> <u>you've</u> <u>always</u> <u>got</u>!

50 IN 50.

If your customers want to buy rocks... <u>then start digging</u>!

Most marketers are trying too hard to sell people the things that <u>they</u> want to sell... **instead of just selling what their market wants to buy.**

Seasoned marketers are the <u>most</u> guilty of this. They believe their marketing skills are powerful enough to sell anything to anyone!

50 IN 50.

Another powerful "secret" from Dan Kennedy.

On Dan's "Renegade Millionaire" program he says:

"You __must__ work on yourself as hard or even harder than you work on your business."

I <u>instantly</u> pulled my car off the road, wrote this down, and have been thinking about it ever since. You should, too. There is so much truth in this one statement – especially if you have been in business for many years. So many seasoned entrepreneurs tell me in private that they have lost their passion for the business that they once had. I've felt this way, too. When you reach this stage in your entrepreneurial life, working on yourself becomes <u>even more important</u>. *You must keep finding all kinds of ways to fire yourself up and keep the flames burning hot!*

50 IN 50.

$ $ $ $ $

The more HONEST and OPEN you are with your customers, the more <u>BONDED</u> they will be to you and the more they'll buy!

People are sick and tired of all the phony-sounding B.S. out there. THEY DON'T TRUST ANYONE ANYMORE. They are looking for something "<u>REAL</u>" and want to have a relationship with you. The more you do to tell them your carefully crafted "personal and private" details, the more money you'll make.

Try this and prove it to yourself!

$ $ $ $ $

50 IN 50.

When people pay –
they **pay** **attention!**

50 IN 50.

Great Marketers
are Hunters.

We are happiest when we're on the hunt. The bigger the hunt – the happier we are. *We must be reaching all the time.* **All is well as long as our reach exceeds our grasp.**

50 IN 50.